Garden Heaven

Vanessa Berridge

Garden Heaven

Inspiration and Escapism for Every Gardener

 National Trust

Published by National Trust Books
An imprint of HarperCollins Publishers
1 London Bridge Street, London SE1 9GF
www.harpercollins.co.uk

First published 2024
© National Trust Books 2024
Text © Vanessa Berridge 2024

HarperCollins Publishers, Macken House
39/40 Mayor Street Upper, Dublin 1
D01 C9W8, Ireland

ISBN 978-0-00-864138-2

10 9 8 7 6 5 4 3 2 1

Previous page The Cut Flower Borders in the Walled Garden at Wallington in Northumberland grow to a height of 8 or 9 feet by late summer. Planting that includes knautias, eryngiums and campanulas is staked with hazel from the wider estate.

Right In early autumn, the sloping Fellside Border at Holehird in the Lake District is a tapestry of persicarias, bergenias, lilac-berried *Gaultheria sinensis* and acers, with the distinctive bare branches of a *Sorbus vilmorinii* in the distance.

Contents

Introduction

'The garden reconciles human art and wild nature, hard work and deep pleasure, spiritual practice and the material world. It is a magical place because it is not divided.'

Thomas Moore (1779–1852)

Garden visiting is one of life's great pleasures. It's a joy to step outside one's routine and wander for a while in a heavenly green space, to look over a magnificent landscape, or withdraw into a beautiful walled garden. Think of carpets of daffodils and bluebells in spring, of high summer borders brimming with colour and scent, and of lavender humming with bees. Or the crunch of frosted twigs on an autumn walk beneath a golden canopy of woodland trees. Good gardens employ all the senses and stimulate an interaction between the visitor and the garden's creator. Understanding what goes into making a garden deepens the experience of any visit.

As Irish writer Thomas Moore suggested, gardening unites many aspects of human endeavour – the practical, the aesthetic, the cerebral and the physical. The creation of a garden is a process of negotiation: with weather, soil, position, wildlife and nature in general. Gardeners need an eye for colour, shape and texture, a retentive memory for plant names, and the willingness to be out in all weathers. I have met gardeners and garden owners across the United Kingdom during my research: through their combination of these qualities, they have helped achieve the outstanding results featured in this book.

These talented people have enthusiastically shared their wealth of knowledge with me. In a modest way, I hope to pass on some of that wisdom, for even imposing gardens have lessons that can be adapted by those of us with rather smaller patches. If you look closely at the detail within a grand scheme, you can learn about successful plant associations or how, for instance, to weave annuals among perennials and shrubs. This book aims to combine escapism with inspiration, to show readers how gardens can

take them into a different world. They can find repose in the view across a lake as blue as the sky, or excitement in the intense colours of a packed border. Readers will be introduced to gardens, both large and small, famous and less familiar. Whatever their differences, all these gardens offer extraordinary beauty at which to marvel and an array of planting styles to provide every gardener with fresh ideas. As you walk round, stop and talk: gardeners are generous people and always happy to offer tips.

Britain has an abundance of glorious gardens thanks to its temperate, forgiving climate. It has been hard to make a selection and I confess freely that my choice is partial and personal,

with several favourites sneaked in. The chapter headings are pointers to the types of garden you will find within these pages. There are romantic flower-filled plots, gardens that fuse with the hills, woods and water surrounding them, and others that look inward within their walls. Gardens featured span centuries of British history: from geometric topiary at Levens Hall created in the 1690s, to Trentham, with its European steppe planting laid out in the early 2000s. Some of the gardens have been in the same family for many years, with skills handed down from generation to generation. Several have national plant collections, and one (Holker Hall) has a 400-year-old lime. Gardens vary

Opposite The legendary Topiary Garden at Levens Hall in Cumbria dates from the late 17th century. In summer, the clipped yew shapes are underplanted with annuals, including *Antirrhinum* 'Liberty Classic Yellow' and golden agastache.

Right Shaped yew pillars act like partitions between different areas of planting within the Rose Garden at Mottisfont in Hampshire. Clipped lavender-edged beds are filled with old single-flowering roses and with perennials chosen to extend the season of interest.

Below At Trentham in Staffordshire, the backdrop to jubilant summer planting of rudbeckias, grasses, helianthus and aconitum is the night-green hillside of King's Wood, a Site of Special Scientific Interest.

from a vast acreage (Bodnant, for example) to a miniature recreation of a Far Eastern landscape at Branklyn in a residential Scottish street.

Certain themes emerged, the most obvious being the drive towards naturalism, even in formal settings. Gardeners today mostly respond to the soil and aspect of their site rather than shoehorning plants into unnatural conditions as was once the fashion. But even in a naturalistic garden, there is still an element of choice: at Wildside in Devon, the gardener physically created different plant habitats in a confronting

fusion of the natural and the artificial. Many gardens now have wildflower meadows, partly to allow nature to take its course, but sometimes through necessity. Cholmondeley's lawns became meadows when furlough during the pandemic left no staff to mow the grass. At Nymans, the wildflower meadow is a Site of Special Scientific Interest, while Great Dixter's long season of plants for pollination has turned it into a hotbed of biodiversity.

Conservation and tradition are often balanced with contemporary design ideas and a widening

Opposite Wildside in Devon features grasses such as *Stipa tenuissima*. Orange, yellow and red daylilies, crocosmia and coreopsis contrast with the many agapanthus varieties just beginning to flower.

Right The Rose Garden at Nymans in West Sussex is a 1990s recreation. Ramblers, including *Rosa* 'Débutante' (foreground), 'François Juranville' (middle) and 'Adélaïde d'Orléans' (back), foam over pergolas and up obelisks, and through lavender-edged beds.

planting palette triggered by climate change. The latter has offered challenges but also opportunities, as has been shown at East Ruston Old Vicarage in Norfolk, where tender plants remain out all winter, and at Hidcote on the north Cotswold escarpment, where drought-tolerant planting now flourishes.

During my visits, I have experienced everything from late frost to unblinking summer sun. One day was so wet I had to return to the garden's entrance to replace the map disintegrating in my hands. But, come sunshine or showers, every garden has delighted and astounded. I have been amazed by the standards of horticulture, often upheld by very few gardeners. I have enjoyed watching the seasons wax and wane, starting out with snowdrops in flower and finishing as the leaves were turning an autumnal gold. I have revisited gardens I knew well and discovered new treasures, and have listened to intriguing stories behind every garden. I hope I have captured the thrill of this journey of discovery and that this book will encourage readers to explore some of these great British gardens for themselves.

A High Romance

Enchanted worlds of colour, scent and texture

Previous page The Main Perennial Border at Wollerton Old Hall, Shropshire, is 16 feet deep. In late summer, the rear is dominated by *Helianthus* 'Lemon Queen', the middle by *Salvia involucrata* 'Bethellii' and *S. atrocyanea*. In front is a mixture of lower-growing salvias, dahlias and hemerocallis.

Opposite Lutyens' new wing, built in sympathy with the original 15th-century house, forms the backdrop to the Long Border. The border is a constantly changing feast of phlox, poppies, daisies and lychnis with shrubs that include *Cotinus coggygria* Rubrifolius Group.

Great Dixter, East Sussex

A visit to Great Dixter in the Sussex Weald is immersive, especially in high summer when everything flowers at head height: narrow pathways squeeze between voluptuous beds and curving yew hedging; annuals mix with perennials; cotoneaster is outlined against yew; shrubs, ferns and ivy jumble together; and wildflower meadows meet the garden borders. There is layer upon layer of interest in a jubilant riot of colour, form and texture – apparently effortless but gardened for over a century with extreme care.

At the garden's heart is a timber-framed, 15th-century house bought in 1910 by Nathaniel Lloyd. The architect Edwin Lutyens integrated within the structure an early 16th-century yeoman's house, brought derelict from nearby Benenden in Kent, and added a sympathetic new wing. Lutyens also designed a rose garden, while Nathaniel laid out the Sunk Garden, and planted the yew hedging and famous bird topiary. His wife, Daisy, made the Long Border.

It was here that Christopher Lloyd was born in 1921, the youngest of six. After Cambridge, five years in the Royal Artillery, and a BSc in horticulture and time teaching at Wye College in Kent, Christopher returned to Great Dixter permanently in 1954. Between then and his death in 2006, he made his parents' garden his own. A plantsman rather than a designer, he built on their foundations and planted within their framework.

Lloyd was never afraid to defy fashion. He planted dazzling colours when most gardeners preferred pastels; a wildflower meadow was the entrance to the garden long before every Chelsea Flower Show garden featured cow parsley and daisies; and he dared dig up Lutyens' rose garden to replace diseased roses with fleshy exotics including tree ferns and palms. Lloyd wrote weekly for *Country Life* magazine and published books, charting his changes and putting his head above the parapet – and was roundly criticised. But he created a garden of remarkable individuality, which since his death in 2006 has been maintained in the same character by Fergus Garrett, head gardener alongside Christopher from 1993 and now CEO of the Great Dixter Charitable Trust.

Left Christopher Lloyd was always more interested in contrast than harmony and his style is still followed today. Bright red poppies and blue cornflowers are mixed with purple *Silene armeria* against the brick walls coped with Kentish peg tiles that are so much a feature of Great Dixter.

Below Flagstone paths run through dense planting in the Cat Garden adjacent to the house. Silver-leafed *Plectranthus argentatus*, euphorbia and ferns are a cool contrast to more colourful planting of a sweet William (*Dianthus* 'Amazon Neon Purple') and *Ageratum houstonianum* 'Blue Horizon'.

Lloyd was a teacher, and education is integral to Great Dixter's work. 'We have fun, learning together as a team, while educating people to think for themselves and encouraging them to break free from shackles,' explains Fergus. 'Why not put orange with pink? Christo always gardened with curiosity and gusto – trying different plant combinations; working out how to mimic nature. Our prime aim is still to be exciting to people.'

Christo always gardened with curiosity and gusto – trying different plant combinations; working out how to mimic nature. Our prime aim is still to be exciting to people.

'Gusto' is the word that comes to mind on a hot summer's day when there are delicious juxtapositions. The welcoming meadow – spangled with ox-eye daisies, yellow ragwort, meadowsweet and orchid spears – swirls round old fruit trees against a dark yew hedge. Arresting and unconventional containers by the front porch combine sedums, stripy grasses and tall blue echiums with viburnum, a fig tree and blue cypress.

In the Barn and Sunk Gardens, the planting is so full as to be almost opaque. Honesty, lupins, poppies, delphiniums, daisies, foxgloves and salvias grow with taller shrubs, bamboo and clematis pyramids. Gardeners are clearing away spring flowerers to make way for late summer annuals. 'I want to champion integrating annuals into the borders,' says Fergus. 'I love bedding out, as long as it's sustainable, which it is here: we make our own compost, collect our own seed and reuse every pot.'

The Long Border, one of Dixter's most recognisable features – yet always adapting – faces over a field of drifting umbellifers and buttercups from which it is separated by a strip of mown grass and a flagstone path laid over a century ago. From benches under an old mulberry tree, you can look along the border

Above The peacock topiary was originally planted by Christopher's father, Nathaniel Lloyd, in the early 20th century. It is now surrounded by relaxed, naturalistic planting that includes *Gladiolus byzantinus*, allium seedheads, verbascum, cornflowers and daisies.

Opposite Great Dixter owes much of its biodiversity to the meadows surrounding the formal garden and is self-sown with yellow rattle, *Leucanthemum vulgare* and other wild flowers that peak in June.

at the textural and colour contrasts. Evergreen shrubs blend with black elder, tall silvery cardoons, roses, herbaceous perennials, grasses and self-seeded umbellifers and poppies.

From the Loggia, supported by eight columns of edge-on red tiles, you can see miscellaneous shapes and drifting grasses in the Topiary Lawn.

Behind, in the Blue Garden are rodgersias, hydrangeas and bergenias shaded by a magnolia, and an assortment of sun-loving annuals in pots.

Non-native plants grow happily alongside natives at Great Dixter, which gives back to nature as much as it takes. A 2012 biodiversity audit showed the garden to be the richest part of the Dixter estate. One hundred and eight species of bees, 32 of butterflies and 77 of lichen have been recorded there. 'We have many habitats, including wet and dry walls and nesting places, and a long season of pollen and nectar because of the variety of our planting,' says Fergus. 'It's not a simple question of rewilding, but a mosaic of different approaches. We are all in this together, and Great Dixter shows how ornamental gardens can play their part.'

Mottisfont, Hampshire

The River Test is as much a feature of Mottisfont as its centuries-old trees, rolling lawns, walled rose garden and fragrant winter woodland. Racing alongside the garden, the pellucid chalk stream is joined by a light cascade of water bubbling up from a spring in the font that gives the estate its name. The early 13th-century priory was dissolved in the 1530s by Henry VIII: its only visible traces are ivy-covered remnants of flint and stone walls on the South Lawn. Somewhere within the graceful stone and brick Georgian house, transformed from a Tudor mansion in the 1740s, the church nave lies hidden.

Ancient oaks, 18th-century sweet chestnuts, purple and green beech, holm oak, hornbeam, the tulip tree *Liriodendron tulipifera* and Indian bean tree *Catalpa speciosa* all contribute to a romantic landscape where meadow, woodland, park and gardens merge.

Lawns incline towards the river past three majestic London plane trees, cushioned in late spring by a mass of white-flowered, frothy umbellifers. The house is anchored by pleached limes, including an allée on the north side designed by leading 20th-century landscape architect Geoffrey Jellicoe. He also planted the lawn below with a succession of yew-buttressed beds and yew columns edged by clipped lavender.

Tucked into the front of the house on the south side is a box parterre, designed by Norah Lindsay in 1938 to reflect the mansion's architecture. Both Jellicoe and Lindsay were guests of society hostess Maud Russell and her banker husband, Gilbert, who bought Mottisfont in 1934. Other guests included the novelist Ian Fleming, and another garden designer, Russell Page, who advised on the planting; some of his suggested shrubs, one of them a rare myrtle, still flourish in the woodland.

Among groves of hazel, cupressus and birches is the Winter Garden. Fragrance comes from winter-flowering viburnum and mahonia, texture from clusters of hellebores, the white ghost bramble *Rubus thibetanus* 'Silver Fern' and dark red berberis, and stem colour from yellow and red dogwoods. The scene is enhanced by pure white, multi-stemmed Himalayan birch *Betula utilis* var. *jacquemontii*, the peeling red

bark of the North Chinese red birch (*B. albosinensis* var. *septentrionalis*) and a gleaming red Tibetan cherry (*Prunus serrula*), while the sun lights up the bark of the evergreen Bhutan pine *Pinus wallichiana* like flames, and its young cones like candles.

Maud Russell handed Mottisfont and the 2,000-acre estate to the National Trust in 1957. In the 1970s, rosarian Graham Stuart Thomas, gardens advisor to the National Trust (1955–75), found a home in the walled garden for his collection of endangered, old-fashioned roses. Plantings of bulbs, perennials and shrubs are complemented by the early season, scented 'Dunwich Rose', a beautiful spiky-stemmed rose covered with poached-egg-like, single flowers.

The garden is a vision of shrubs and standards, ramblers and climbers, rugosa, damask and centifolia, the sweet briar or Eglantine rose and hybrid perpetuals. Apricot 'Ghislaine de Féligonde' and 'Violacea' entwine themselves in knotted old apple trees, remnants from kitchen garden days. Pinky-white 'Francis E. Lester' and violet blue 'Veilchenblau' ramble over arches, while tiny pink *Rosa* 'Blush Noisette' flowers appear against sun-reflecting walls. The sweet briar 'Manning's Blush' dates from before 1797, and the dark red, thornless 'Souvenir du Docteur Jamain', a hybrid perpetual, from 1865. Over

The sun lights up the bark of the evergreen Bhutan pine like flames, and its young cones like candles.

Opposite A visitor's first glimpse is of three great plane trees, which create a magnificent framework for the Georgian mansion. Probably dating from the early 19th century, the trees are softened with umbellifer cushions.

Right Candelabra pear trees are a reminder that this was once a kitchen garden. Verbascum, foxgloves and irises intermingle with shrub pink *Rosa* x *centifolia* 'De Meaux' and a pink Portland rose.

Below right The garden is fragrant in summer with the scent of single-flowering old roses including *R.* 'La Ville de Bruxelles', white *R.* 'Leda', and variegated red and white *R.* x *damascena* 'Versicolor' and *R.* 'Oeillet Parfait'.

a pergola climb 'Bleu Magenta' and rose-pink 'Débutante', a 1902 rambling rose. Standards of 'Little White Pet' and light magenta Portland rose, 'Comte de Chambord', stand in pools of compact, silver-leafed santolina. There are waxy-leafed roses and those with narrow leaves set along spiny stems, roses that grow in tight shrubs and others in great loose sprays.

This scintillating variety gives the Rose Garden its special place at Mottisfont, while the magnificent ancient trees (its great plane tree is thought to be the largest in Britain), winter inspiration, refined riverside setting and romantic house mark Mottisfont out for year-round appeal.

Nymans, West Sussex

Nymans shimmers in June heat. The wildflower meadow, abuzz with bees and butterflies, runs down dreamily to parkland, beyond which the leafy High Weald, an Area of Outstanding Natural Beauty, is a soft grey smudge on a cloudless day.

Ludwig Messel, a German émigré banker of Jewish descent, enticed by those countryside views, bought the West Sussex estate with 300 acres of woodland in 1890. Over the quarter century before his death in 1915, Ludwig laid down the bones of the 33-acre garden that would go on to be enhanced by his descendants: his late grand-daughter, Anne, wrote that Nymans mirrors 'a glimpse from each generation, that time and growth have moulded into a harmonious whole'.

A visitor today is conscious of that harmony. Red brick walls and yew and laurel hedging are not hard and fast divisions but invitations to explore further. Enclosed, plant-packed areas yield to extensive lawns and the enveloping Sussex landscape.

Ludwig was partly inspired by his Sussex neighbours: at what proved a key moment in British gardening, Wilfred Loder was making a woodland and water garden at High Beeches, William Robinson was promoting a new naturalism at Gravetye Manor, and Stephenson Robert Clarke was establishing his tree and shrub collection at Borde Hill (see pp. 150– 154). Ludwig started with the Pinetum in 1892, grouping families of conifers, and then planted the Arboretum of oaks, limes and birches in a damp area between the garden and woodland.

In the garden itself, Ludwig and then his son, Leonard, established rarities sent home by plant hunters such as Ernest Wilson and George Forrest, and also bred new cultivars, a tradition still honoured at Nymans. Their head gardener's plant-hunting son, Harold Comber, introduced to the UK species from South America, including the Chilean myrtle (*Luma apiculata*). These are still in the Wall Garden, created as a trial ground from a former orchard.

At the Wall Garden's heart, Ludwig installed a marble fountain encircled by four yew chess-pieces, and planted what has become a lofty

Davidia involucrata, otherwise known as the handkerchief tree for its striking, late spring flowerheads, along with magnolias, camellias and rhododendrons. In June, the flowering Chinese dogwood (*Cornus kousa*) becomes a focus with great clouds of creamy white (*C. k.* 'John Slocock'), and rich apricot-pink (*C. k.* 'Miss Satomi') bracts.

Ludwig's other projects included the Rock Garden, restored between 2016 and 2022 in a process that current head gardener Joe Whelan describes as 'part archaeology, part gardening'. Rocky stepping stones were excavated and new plantings were made in sandstone hewn from a local quarry. Rocks studded with dianthus, rock roses and a waterfall of thymes recall the garden's Edwardian heyday.

> Rocks studded with dianthus, rock roses and a waterfall of thymes recall the garden's Edwardian heyday.

Leonard filled the Top Garden with more magnolias and rhododendrons. These still give depth to the pastel June Borders that are visible from both the path and from the glades behind. The Rose Garden, originally made in the 1920s by Leonard's wife, Maud, has since been moved and reworked; it is now planted with repeat-flowering David Austin roses around nepeta, honeysuckle and yews.

Opposite A magnificent cedar of Lebanon towers over the recently restored Rock Garden. A small Japanese shrine evokes the Far East from which many plants were introduced.

Right Drought-tolerant plants thrive in the stony Rock Garden. Planting includes carmine pink dianthus, *Acer palmatum* var. *dissectum*, *Kalmia latifolia* 'Ostbo Red', santolina, cistus, lavender and hebe species and cultivars.

Below The wildflower meadows flow out from the garden towards the parkland and woodland beneath a spreading copper beech. The meadow is a Site of Special Scientific Interest.

The Great Storm of 1987 felled 80 per cent of the trees in the Pinetum. Survivors include two towering coastal redwoods, nicknamed Bill and Ben, now underplanted with new introductions, including *Acer palmatum*. The concern for rare species continues: an etiolated Chinese swamp cypress, *Glyptostrobus pensilis*. is given attention. 'It doesn't look impressive,' says Joe, 'but it's now dying out in the wild.'

The ancient wildflower meadow is a Site of Special Scientific Interest. It is studded with native species, including knapweed, trefoil, yellow rattle and common spotted orchids, which grow tall in the shade of the lime avenue that runs off the meadow. The meadow is cut with a mechanical scythe in August and the resulting hay laid on other wildflower areas to allow for seeding.

Today's taste for a more relaxed style of gardening can also be seen in the Sunken Garden, where a Byzantine urn is surrounded by clouds of *Alchemilla mollis* and *Geranium* 'Johnson's Blue' rather than by carpet bedding. In the Forecourt,

Above In the once formal Forecourt, plants are now allowed to spill over and self-seeders encouraged. Peachy *Rosa* 'Alister Stella Gray' along the wall is the backdrop to meadow-style beds of scabious, cirsium, ragged robin (*Lychnis flos-cuculi*), marguerites and larkspur.

roses and pyramidal lollipops of yew are planted with cottage garden favourites scabious, cirsium, ragged robin, marguerites and larkspur.

'We think about the impact on wildlife when we rework an area of the garden,' says Joe. A beech tree destroyed by root rot, for example, has been reduced to a craggy monolith over which *Rosa* 'Paul's Himalayan Musk' now climbs. It has become a home for birds and insects, as well as being aesthetically pleasing. The development of this historic estate continues with a sympathetic touch.

Polesden Lacey, Surrey

Years ago, I attended an open-air performance at Polesden Lacey. During the second act, there was early applause. It took me a while to realise that it wasn't the audience, but bats, attracted by the stage lights, beating their wings in the pines behind. This kind of magic is endemic to

Polesden Lacey with its avenues of ancient trees, yew walks, walled Rose Garden and magnificent Edwardian house, all set against Surrey hills wooded with oak, beech and birch.

If anything, that romance has now been enhanced by more relaxed management. Chalk grasslands compacted by frequent mowing have been returned to wildflower meadows spread out beneath limes, weeping elms, walnuts and cherries. Naturalised daffodils start the season, followed by camassias, then buttercups, umbellifers, clover and speedwell, with bee orchids in high summer. Only when the wild flowers have completely died down in late July are the meadows given their annual mow. Even the South Lawn is now left semi-wild, studded with daisies, buttercups and clover and marrying the garden with the landscape beyond.

A 350-year-old avenue of sweet chestnuts leads to the mansion that was home from 1907 to Margaret Greville, who bequeathed the estate to the Trust in 1942. The daughter of a Scottish brewer, Mrs Greville rose to the pinnacle of British society, and numbered

King Edward VII among her house-party guests. In 1923, the future King George VI and Queen Elizabeth spent their honeymoon at Polesden Lacey. Photographs show them playing golf on the lawns and strolling along a waist-high yew walk – now a towering dark tunnel.

Mrs Greville is still a presence at Polesden Lacey. She is buried in the Lady's Garden, bounded by yew hedging and brick walls and by a border of *Alchemilla mollis*, while, tucked among trees, is her pets' graveyard. In the 1920s, she created the 18th-century-style Long Walk for her visitors to appreciate the view of woods and fields rising up to Ranmore Common (also under National Trust care, and supplying chestnut poles and woodchips to the garden). Lion-topped pillars wound with roses mark the opening of a walk lined by elbow-high hedging and indented by a series of three urns on pedestals inscribed with quotations from the 18th-century poet and satirist, Alexander Pope. One comes from his translation of Homer's *Iliad*: 'Where not a breath disturbs the deep serene.'

Lion-topped pillars wound with roses mark the opening of a walk lined by elbow-high hedging and indented by a series of three urns on pedestals.

Mrs Greville also laid out the Rose Garden in 1910–11 within the 18th-century flint and brick walls of a former vegetable garden. An Arts and Crafts-style pergola runs through the centre, underplanted with low euonymus hedging. This

remains a formal, old-fashioned rose garden with beds of recently reinvigorated shrub roses set in four square lawns. In June, the garden is fragrant with climbers and ramblers on the pergola. The season is prolonged by wall-backed beds with further climbing and shrub roses, here combined with perennials, bulbs, bearded irises and shrubs, including the dramatic smoke bush *Cotinus coggygria* 'Royal Purple': on an October day, after a shower, raindrops glisten on its purple-bronze leaves.

In May, the Peony Border, pitted with *Allium* 'Purple Sensation', and the Iris Border, both also within the walled garden, come into their own. An armillary sphere stands in a central octagonal bed of pale lavender-blue *Iris pallida* var. *dalmatica*, surrounded by further plantings of different coloured irises. This is the season, too, when many of the trees flower, including several fuchsia-pink Judas trees (*Cercis siliquastrum*) and a *Davidia involucrata*, festooned with its pocket-handkerchief blooms in the Sunken Garden.

Outside the walls, the Herbaceous Borders take up the story in summer. Shrubs provide a backdrop to roses, daisy-flowered *Leucanthemum × superbum* 'Alaska', kniphofias, veronicastrum, bright *Helenium* 'Moerheim Beauty', grasses and spiky *Acanthus mollis*. In December and January – the garden is open all year – the Winter Garden is scented by flowering shrubs including mahonia and sweet box *Sarcococca*.

Polesden Lacey is a grand garden that teeters on the point of returning to the wild. The felling of overcrowded trees to give space to the most important specimens is being masterminded by head gardener Natan Cointet. He joined Polesden Lacey from the clay of Scotney Castle, Kent, in March 2023, and enjoys working with the very different soil. He plans to introduce wild plants from the wider estate into the thinned-out woodlands around the house.

Rather as National Trust houses open in winter to exhibit more rarely seen restoration work, so Natan sees the potential of opening up wider areas as they are cleared and replanted. 'I want visitors to share in the garden's evolution and feel like guests,' says Natan.

Opposite One of the glories of Polesden Lacey is its setting. The lawns run seamlessly away from the mansion towards wooded National Trust land running up to Ranmore Common.

Right The planting in the southerly Herbaceous Border is backed by low yew hedging that gives a sharp outline to a mixture of agapanthus, verbascum, hollyhocks and other cottage garden favourites.

Below Elegant stone urns on pedestals flank the entrances to the flamboyantly Edwardian-style Herbaceous Borders, which, at 492ft, are among the longest in the UK.

Opposite The Cottage Garden enfolds South Cottage, with planting in bright reds and yellows set against four bulging Irish yew pillars. Stone and brick paths are bordered by verbascums, poppies, achillea and Martagon lilies.

Sissinghurst Castle Garden, Kent

For Vita Sackville-West and husband Harold Nicolson, Sissinghurst was a place of high romance: the ruins of a 16th-century castle set amid its own woods, farmland and streams, and with uninterrupted views over Kent. Unable as a woman to inherit Knole, her childhood home in Sevenoaks, Vita found consolation at Sissinghurst Castle and in the making of a garden around the restored buildings of their unusual property.

Already a prolific published author, it was Vita's writing of her garden through her *Observer* column in the 1950s that cemented the reputation of Sissinghurst. Her husband and co-creator, Harold Nicolson, also wrote: his diaries brought to life British politics from 1930, the year that the Nicolsons bought Sissinghurst Castle. The diaries shed light on the garden's creation and the strength of the couple's unorthodox partnership.

Fascinated by the private worlds of these public figures, revealed through their writings, Sissinghurst has remained one of my favourite gardens, for the characters of the people who

> Vita and Harold's partnership balanced his sense of design with her love of plants often chosen for their historical or literary associations.

created it are still reflected in both its formation and in its planting: 'My liking for gardens to be lavish is an inherent part of my garden philosophy,' wrote Vita. 'I like generosity wherever I find it, whether in gardens or elsewhere.'

Vita and Harold's partnership balanced his sense of design with her love of plants often chosen for their historical or literary associations. The tension between those aspects contributes to Sissinghurst's charm, with Harold influenced by the gardens of Persia that he had seen as a young diplomat. It was Harold who provided the setting for Vita's planting: he planned the Yew Walk that runs parallel with the Long Library and connects the Rose Garden to the White

Garden; the red brick walls that enclose ebullient planting; and the yew roundel that acts as a green pause within the flamboyant Rose Garden. Yew pillars give definition to hot yellows, oranges and reds around Harold's South Cottage. There are avenues – the Nuttery, the pleached Lime Walk and azalea-lined Moat Walk, resplendent in spring – that in summer contrast with abundance elsewhere. The lawns of the Front Court are offset by the packed Purple Border of sweet peas, cerinthe, dark poppies, geraniums and antirrhinums, *Salvia nemorosa* 'Caradonna', buddleia and purple hesperis.

The legendary White Garden was laid out with box hedging and brick paths in the 1940s. In June, its central dome of *Rosa mulliganii* rises above uncompromisingly white planting of annuals and bulbs, changed according to the season.

Texture is important, too: there's the warm red brick of the walls and buildings, the alternation between grass, stone flags, red brick and herringbone tiles for the paths. One of the best views in high summer is looking back at the 16th-century tower (where Vita had her writing room), proud above the fruit trees, umbellifers and long grass in the Orchard. It seems as if both

garden and castle have arisen organically from Kent farmland.

Pamela Schwerdt and Sybille Kreutzberger joined Vita in 1959 as joint head gardeners. They oversaw the garden's transition to the National Trust in 1967, and, according to Adam Nicolson, Vita's grandson, 'in their refinement and heightening over three decades of the ideas which Vita and Harold had begun here, they should be seen as joint creators of the garden'. Troy Scott Smith has worked on and off at Sissinghurst since 1992, most recently returning as head gardener in 2022.

In most Trust gardens, particularly one as historic as Sissinghurst, there are arguments about how development should be squared with preservation. Troy says time away helps: 'You come back with different reflections. You can't stop the clock but we are still trying to present

Above A Gothic-style pergola submerged by *Rosa mulliganii* is the central feature of the White Garden. Planting changes through the seasons, with marguerites, lilies and foxgloves for high summer.

Vita Sackville-West's garden. It had become a bit too perfect at one time.'

Vita was every inch a countrywoman and Troy believes that recent innovations, such as planting corncockles and ox-eye daisies in the Rose Garden, help return the garden to Vita's ethos. He eventually hopes to bring cows into the meadow by the entrance and show that Sissinghurst is 'a functioning landscape rather than just a tourist attraction'. Like all National Trust gardens, Sissinghurst is gardened sustainably, roses aren't sprayed and nothing is watered (even in the 2022 drought) apart from

pots and new plantings. 'We are building more resilience into the soil.' The Front Court lawn is mulch mowed (grass cuttings left on the surface after mowing) and is springy turf rather than the bowling green I recall from past visits.

In 2019, the Delos garden was reinstated by walls near the Priest's House. Inspired by a trip to the Greek island in 1935, this area of the garden aimed to reproduce Delos's atmosphere and arid landscape, but ultimately failed because Vita and Harold struggled with Mediterranean planting over cold, wet winters. Now, pillars of a ruined temple once again stand on a gentle elevation above stone ruins and shepherds' walls made from the same Kentish ragstone used for centuries at Sissinghurst. All the plants –

dianthus, fennel, sages, phlomis, cistus – are found growing in Greece, only now they are suitable for Britain's hotter, dryer summers too.

Different in feel from the rest of the garden, Delos shows how the past can be reclaimed to suit new climatic conditions. Vita hated the thought of her garden leaving the family ('so long as I live no Nat Trust or any other foreign body shall have my darling', she wrote), but her legacy is conserved and her spirit lives on amid the beautiful landscape she treasured.

Opposite Delos's difference in style surprises many visitors. In fact, it is a 2019 reimagining of an earlier, Mediterranean-style garden that failed because of harsh winters in the 1930s and 1940s.

Right Climate change allows tender planting that once struggled at Sissinghurst to succeed now in rough stone and gravel. Planting includes ballota, sages, salsify, euphorbia and achillea.

Below The view over the Rose Garden from Vita's tower reveals the blending of Harold's design and Vita's plantsmanship. The yew roundel is reflected in the shape of the half-moon brick wall at one end. Lavish beds of roses and perennials are lined by winter-flowering cherries.

Wollerton Old Hall, Shropshire

The story itself is romantic: Lesley Jenkins lived at Wollerton Old Hall as a child, and then bought the house in the early 1980s with her husband, John. 'There was nothing here from my childhood,' says Lesley. 'It was just a field of cows.' But when it came to creating a garden, the Jenkinses felt that it needed to be formal to match the beautiful, half-timbered, 16th-century house, and so devised a strong linear layout, based initially on three north–south and three east–west vistas.

Gradually, over 40 years, Lesley and John have pushed the garden out over 3.5 acres, creating some 16 semi-secret rooms – building walls, planting hedges and laying paths of grass, stone, gravel and herringbone brick to vary the pace of a walk round the garden. Domes, pyramids and roundels of box and yew unite areas of quite distinct planting.

From the house, straight paths lead to a wooden arbour, a planted urn or a gateway. Yet you are constantly tempted to slip sideways,

attracted by breaks in hedging or by glimpses through half-opened doors of concealed rooms. Each garden has its own sense of mystery. 'We wanted to keep the atmosphere of a child's garden,' says Lesley.

One vista is down a grassy avenue of yews. These pyramids are backed by a wall on one side and a beech hedge on the other, and punctuate beds of herbaceous planting and roses. On the far side of the garden is a parallel border of billowing perennials, backed by plumes of fluffy, white, moisture-loving goat's beard (*Aruncus*). In between these two main arteries, and centred on a wing of the house, is a pleached lime allée opening onto a sunken stone courtyard with box balls and Japanese irises (*Iris ensata*) in the central pool of the Lower Rill.

The rill crosses through the pool and between beech hedging. Beyond, it runs between large box balls and a grove of pollarded hornbeam,

with further planting of irises, *Alchemilla mollis* and white wisteria. This introduces a calm note into the general exuberance, as does a grass courtyard enclosed by beech and yew hedges, a wall and a wooden and brick pergola covered with roses and clematis.

There are many wonderful little corners: a sundial stands on a stone plinth at the junction of two grass paths. Ankle-high box hedging contains planting around a circle of gravel, while elsewhere planting spills out on to stone, grass and gravel. Cerise and violet clematis rush over fences, walls and arches. In a damper spot, spires of yellow ligularia form a curtain behind a bench

---

Domes, pyramids and roundels of box and yew unite areas of quite distinct planting.

Above The Oak Gazebo is the backdrop to the Sundial Garden planting, which includes *Aster* x *frikartii* 'Mönch', *Iris* 'English Cottage', *Aconitum* 'Stainless Steel' and *Salvia microphylla* 'Pink Pong'.

Left Looking along the Sundial Garden borders towards the 16th-century house. By late summer, irises, roses, phlox and delphiniums have been overtaken by asters, dahlias and *Salvia* 'Phyllis Fancy', which flowers from July to early November.

Opposite The Lower Rill is surrounded by large balls of yew (*Taxus baccata*). Clumps of *Iris ensata* 'Rose Queen' in the water produce beautiful pink flowers in June, but their strappy leaves create interest and structure later in the year.

between two yew domes – somewhere to admire yet another prospect.

At the bottom of the garden, a brick arch marks the transition to a wilder area known as the Croft. Grassy paths amble through drifts of geraniums and umbellifers beneath a selection of fine trees. The die-straight lines of the main axes disappear not only in the Croft but also in a woodland area of multi-stemmed white birches to one side of the house.

As an artist, Lesley understands the importance of colour and form, apparent from the style and quality of her planting. Stone-edged mixed borders of blues, pinks and whites – delphiniums, roses and *Stachys byzantina* in summer, and asters in September – contrast with the reds, oranges and yellows of late summer favourites – dahlias, heleniums and crocosmias – colours that Lesley favours in her paintings.

Dahlias in reds, oranges and yellows are planted with rudbeckias, heleniums, crocosmias, achilleas and grasses in a room influenced by the late summer planting at Lanhydrock in Cornwall.

Rambling, climbing and shrub roses feature everywhere at Wollerton Old Hall. Lesley's most recent development is a courtyard with mass planting of a pale peachy, myrrh-scented climber, named for the garden by David Austin.

Lesley claims, that like a painting in her studio, 'my garden is never finished'. It is, she says, a very personal space, created for her and John. Nevertheless, she enjoys sharing the garden – and this one delights visitors, working well with its ancient house, yet somehow surprisingly contemporary.

Hills, Woods and Water

Where all nature is a garden

Bodnant Garden, Conwy

Bodnant is a garden without parallel. You know it immediately when you walk through the entrance towards massive borders where hot colours mimic those of tender perennials once grown in glasshouses on this spot. In July, cannas, dahlias and lilies pulsate against berberis and purple cotinus. The setting, too, is unmatched, looking out across the River Conwy to the mountains of Snowdonia.

From late May to early June, the celebrated 1880s laburnum arch is in full bloom, and attracts over 3,300 visitors a day, but with some 80 acres to explore, these numbers are easily absorbed. It is a garden of two halves: the formal lawns and terraces around the Victorian mansion, and the woodlands. Led by Ned Lomax, 28 gardeners are divided into teams responsible for different aspects of the garden and five national collections: *Eucryphia*, *Magnolia*, *Embothrium*, *Rhododendron forrestii* and the special group of *Rhododendron* Bodnant hybrids.

The same family has been at Bodnant since it was bought in 1874 by industrialist, financier and Liberal politician Henry Pochin. And,

from 1920 until 2005, three generations of Puddles – Frederick, Charles and Martin – made their mark as head gardeners. Their hybridising work is commemorated in a garden of Bodnant rhododendrons, chosen from among the 350 they registered. The estate was handed to the National Trust in 1949 but descendants of Pochin's daughter, Laura McLaren, continue to live in the house: great-great-grandson Michael McLaren maintains a committed interest as the current garden director. Bodnant has also been a training ground for National Trust head gardeners: Troy Scott Smith, now at Sissinghurst (see pp. 34–39), led much of the renovation in planting between 2006 and 2013.

The layers of history are evident throughout. Pochin had the East Garden laid out with spacious lawns, intersected by stone paths, steps and balustrades in the fashionable Italian Renaissance style, and now edged with late summer borders. The Round Garden, also dating from the late 19th century, was recently replanted in contemporary prairie style with grasses, achilleas and eryngiums. Dark seedheads

Between 1905 and 1914, Henry created the five west terraces overlooking the Carneddau mountains. The terraces descend dramatically via stone staircases before the land drops away towards the southern woodland slopes.

of *Rudbeckia occidentalis* 'Green Wizard' are left on for winter interest.

Pochin's grandson, Henry, 2nd Baron Aberconway, was put in charge of the garden in 1901 when he was just 21. He became a major figure in British horticulture and was President of the Royal Horticultural Society from 1931 until his death in 1953. Like his friend, Colonel Stephenson Robert Clarke at Borde Hill (see pp. 150–154), he collected exotic introductions from Asia and America, and helped sponsor plant-finding expeditions. He was also interested in hybridisation, and won gold medals at RHS shows.

Between 1905 and 1914, Henry created the five west terraces overlooking the Carneddau mountains. The terraces descend dramatically via stone staircases before the land drops away towards the southern woodland slopes. Built by hand by 100 labourers, the terraces are slightly off the axis of the house, centred instead between a cedar of Lebanon and a blue Atlas cedar, *Cedrus atlantica* 'Glauca', planted by Pochin in 1876.

Next is the Croquet Terrace, with a huge double-stemmed *Magnolia campbellii*, an early introduction by plant collector George Forrest. The two cedars and the mansion are reflected in the still pool on the Lily Terrace, skirted by Bodnant hybrid rhododendrons planted in 2014. The Lower Rose Terrace is an Edwardian confection of pitch pine pergolas and uprights, smothered in climbers, and beds replanted with pink and red David Austin roses. Along

Opposite From the Top Lawn, a path runs between *Pieris formosa* var. *forrestii*, red *Rhododendron* 'Choremia', and pale green *Cercidiphyllum japonica*. Beyond is the Round Garden with a fountain and a border of *Taxus* x *media* 'Hicksii'.

Right The 18th-century Pin Mill, brought from Gloucestershire in 1938, is reflected in the glassy waters of the Canal Terrace. Behind the building, the woodland drops steeply away.

Below The River Hiraethlyn runs at pace through the woodland beneath a series of bridges and over a dam that was renovated in 2012.

Right Behind the Grade II-listed Old Mill, Furnace Hillside rises steeply. It is covered with magnolias and a good collection of rhododendron species grown from seed sent back by plant hunters as well as many Bodnant-raised rhododendron hybrids.

the bottom Canal Terrace is a rhythmic border designed with grasses, climbers, hazel and elder to emulate Welsh hedgerows. At one end is the Pin Mill, built in Gloucestershire in 1730 and then dismantled brick by brick and moved to Bodnant in 1938.

The Deep Bath, part of Pochin's original East Garden, featuring an oval pool within sheltering balustraded walls, was re-formed in 2016 as a tropical garden, with bananas, trachycarpus, hedychiums, cannas, tetrapanax and the foxglove tree *Paulownia tomentosa*, which is stooled hard every year for large jungly leaves.

It is from here that paths wind into the woodlands, with a choice of circuits along which the sound of water is constantly heard. An azalea-lined path from the 1920s curls round past the stream that runs down through the Rockery to the Dell and the Grade II-listed Old Mill, built between 1828 and 1837.

There are steep gradients and perilous drops, and, for the brave, stepping stones, often moss covered, over fast-moving water. The River Hiraethlyn flows through the woodlands, gathering momentum as it heads towards the Conwy. Above its banks rises the Pinetum, part of Pochin's design and planted by his daughter, Laura. Storm Arwen took out 50 mature pines in 2021 and uprooted Bodnant's magnificent coastal redwood, a *Sequoia sempervirens*

Above The Deep Bath is part of the Victorian design, predating the terraces. The make-up of the planting changes from year to year but major components are tetrapanax, bananas (*Musa* and *Ensete*), dahlias and salvias.

champion registered as the tallest in Wales, which wrenched up the river bank as it fell.

The Far End of the garden was developed by Laura between 1895 and 1905 and influenced by naturalist garden pioneer William Robinson. Head gardener Ned feels it has become over-gardened and plans a return to greater naturalism, with grass and the odd shrub at the water's edge, and acers and birches for autumn colour. Off the main route is the Yew Garden, planted with Chinese rhododendrons in an atmospheric tangle of old stems. Some are marked with Ernest Wilson's collecting numbers from the early 1900s.

From one viewpoint, you see Furnace Hill, right on the edge of the estate, enveloped in pines and deciduous trees with a sub-storey of Wilson, Forrest and Kingdon-Ward rhododendrons, which are a patchwork of spring colour. Higher up, you look down through the crowns of the big conifers and oaks on pockets of blue hydrangeas, while on the Waterfall Bridge, the view is downstream into the woodlands or over the damn to the Mill Pond. These quieter moments were beloved of the McLaren family and allow visitors a closer link to the Welsh countryside. You may catch sight of nesting grebes, a heron, dragonflies or even a kingfisher.

Branklyn Garden, Perthshire

Nothing quite prepares you for Branklyn Garden. You duck down a quiet residential street on the outskirts of Perth, then suddenly walk out into a Sino-Himalayan landscape, a feeling intensified on a humid summer's day. Ahead are rocky slopes studded with alpines and groves of acers, halesia, eucryphia and rhododendrons among pines and birches.

At just 1.7 acres, Branklyn is a grand landscape in miniature where Eastern planting is reinterpreted for Britain. Stand in the wooden gazebo beneath a splendid hornbeam for a panorama across the garden – the melding of Branklyn's trees with pine and deciduous woods on the far side of the River Tay links this Far Eastern world with the Perthshire hills. There is a gorgeous variety of planting between lawns, gravel paths, rock gardens, pool and woodlands.

Two grand vistas, cut down to size, lead off the tea lawn: a century-old avenue of *Acer palmatum* 'Dissectum', and a double herbaceous border culminating in a sundial surrounded by flowering shrubs and trees, including a magnolia and rhododendrons. The borders hint at

Gertrude Jekyll's influence in their associations of perennials – astrantias, crocosmias, bergenias, sedums and knautias – with low shrubs, such as pieris and hydrangeas.

These elements were assembled by Dorothy Renton, just 24 when she and her husband, John, moved here following their marriage in 1922. They bought an overgrown, half-acre orchard on which they built an Arts and Crafts house with pantile roof and carved wooden fascia. They cleared the orchard, then acquired more land as Dorothy discovered a passion for plants: of the 3,500 species at Branklyn today almost 50 per cent are direct descendants of ones she acquired.

Dorothy's enthusiasm was partly inspired by the influx in the 1920s of Far Eastern plants,

> The melding of Branklyn's trees with pine and deciduous woods on the far side of the River Tay links this Far Eastern world with the Perthshire hills.

Left An arch made from Tibetan cherry branches leads from the Gertrude Jekyll-inspired border to a sundial, bordered by *Osmanthus delavayi*, *Magnolia* x *loebneri* 'Merrill', *Rhododendron* 'Blue Diamond' and *R. trichanthum*.

Below This spectacular bank is the visitor's introduction to Branklyn. From left to right, it features white *Osmanthus delavayi*, red *Acer palmatum*, pinky *Rhododendron concinnum* and *R. augustinii*.

which she incorporated within a Scottish setting, protected from north and east winds by Kinnoull Hill. John, a land agent, created homes for Dorothy's plants: he terraced the 45-degree slope and designed the three rock gardens and the network of level paths, connected by stone and earth steps.

You can lose yourself in the small-scale woodlands among blue Himalayan poppies in May and June. Paths are edged with epimediums and hostas below a middle tier of perennials, including dainty white *Anemone rivularis* 'Glacier'. Above are trees and shrubs: the eponymous three-stemmed bronze *Prunus serrula* 'Branklyn', white-stemmed birches, dark red *Acer palmatum* 'Atropurpureum' and a fabulous *Hoheria glabrata* (the New Zealand mountain ribbonwood) covered with white flowers in July.

Even in mid-summer the diversity of spring-flowering rhododendrons is attractive. There are small-leafed *Rhododendron* 'Blue Diamond', *R. thomsonii* with peeling bark, and waxy *Rhododendron* 'Carmen'. Another is *Rhododendron roxieanum*, like an inverted candelabra with clusters of narrow, spiky leaves.

The pond and bog garden are planted with astilbes, hostas, water lilies, ferns, primulas and rodgersias and fed by a cascade that springs down over rocks beneath a sprawling cedar of Lebanon, *Cedrus libani* 'Atlantica Aurea'. Above,

in the Alpine and Scree Garden, are pincushions of *Astilbe* 'Willie Buchanan', compact *Rhododendron aureum*, ground-hugging *Sorbus poteriifolia* and low-growing *Daphne × susannae* 'Cheriton' along with minuscule sempervivums, sarracenias and sedums.

When the Rentons died childless in the 1960s, they left Branklyn to the National Trust for Scotland. 'It is an interesting balance between maintaining the legacy of the garden's creators while acknowledging that things change,' says Kate White, head gardener since March 2023. Branklyn's notable peat walls were pioneered here and at the Royal Botanic Garden

Edinburgh in the 1920s, with blocks of peat used to form low retaining walls that provided a moist, well-drained acid environment for plants such as dwarf rhododendrons, primulas and meconopsis. These walls are now maintained and repaired with other less controversial materials in line with the National Trust for Scotland's policy of helping conserve peatlands.

Dorothy Renton's vision lives on through planting that is still guided by the plant accession books she kept for more than 40 years, in which she documented all the garden's acquisitions. As Kate says: 'Dorothy propagated and introduced so many different genera and species that we have a huge range to explore when renovating and restoring plantings.' Dorothy herself wrote: 'The garden … has evolved gradually and the principal aim has been to give the plants the proper conditions – it is primarily a home-from-home for plants.'

Glendurgan Garden, Cornwall

Glendurgan's gardens fit like a glove into a sheltered valley looking out on to the picturesque Helford estuary. Here, exotic trees and shrubs luxuriate in the mild climate of Cornwall's south coast.

Glendurgan Garden was laid out in the 1830s by Alfred Fox (1794–1874), a Quaker shipping agent. Alfred and his wife, Sarah, cleared three overgrown and marshy valleys, dug a large pond and planted lime, beech, pine, oak and holm oak and newly introduced American conifers to create the backdrop to their garden. These windbreaks remain a feature, rising up above camellias, magnolias and rhododendrons.

In 1833, Fox created the laurel maze, based on a late 18th-century design in Sydney Gardens, Bath, and positioned it on an east-facing slope at the heart of the garden. In the centre is a thatched summerhouse, with Chusan palms (*Trachycarpus fortunei*) in each quadrant. The maze captures Glendurgan's spirit: from afar it looks like an Assam tea plantation, yet nearer

> The meadow is cut back in late June and then recut in winter for a velvety spring look with wild violets and pink and yellow primroses.

its neat, clipped formality becomes clearer. It is playful, and easy to get lost in, but also tricky to maintain across both the seasons and the years, particularly in the lower boggy section.

Glendurgan was given to the National Trust in 1962 by the Foxes, but the current generation keeps a weather eye on the garden's development from their house (not open to the public) at the valley's head. The violent storm of 1990 proved a catalyst for investment in the 30-acre garden, explains John Lanyon, head gardener to three of Cornwall's National Trust estates – Glendurgan, Trelissick and Trerice. 'Glendurgan is a very dynamic, forward-looking garden,' says Lanyon, 'with respect for tradition and the genius of its setting.' A major aim has been to define the character of the various areas and distinguish them from one another.

Sun-lovers grow at the entrance: grey, spiky agaves and puyas, grassy restio and elegia, a palm from Easter Island, New Zealand *Pachystegia insignis* (waxy-leafed groundcover) and South African *Banksia coccinea*, with its sensational red and white striped flowers in late April. This segues into a Cornish grove of camellias, offering a radiant, early season mix of red, pink and cream.

Rhythmic variations in the planting are marked by individual trees: at one junction by an ancient oak, at another by a towering purple beech. A huge tulip tree, planted by Fox in the 1830s, braces its muscular branches like a prize fighter over a wildflower meadow. The meadow

Left In early May, natural drifts of indigenous bluebells (*Hyacinthoides non-scripta*) flow beneath flowering cherries, tall pines and rhododendrons.

Below A deep grass valley runs down through one side of the garden, planted with bluebells, *Dicksonia antarctica* and pale *Rhododendron* x 'Loderi'.

Opposite Dappled spring sunlight plays on a bluebell-covered hillside through the branches of the fine old parkland trees that are one of the features of Glendurgan.

is cut back in late June and then recut in winter for a velvety spring look with wild violets, pink and yellow primroses and, later in the season, six types of native orchid. Bluebells carpet the banks in May, representing natural Cornwall among overseas exotics.

Micro-climates create further variation in the length of the valley. Winding down paths edged by bullies (long local cobble stones) to the sea at Durgan village, you move from open banks, planted with South African protea, banksia, dierama and grevillea, through groves of rhododendrons and camellias. Large-leafed foliage plants from New Zealand, introduced since the 1990s, are shaded by trees, which include the endangered New Zealand kauri *Agathis australis*, with a dark greenish-brown, ribbed trunk. Magnolias are protected from frost along the floor of the valley with the Asiatic species, including *Magnolia campbellii*, *M. sprengeri* and *M. sargentiana* var. *robusta*, flowering early, with large pink, mauve or white tepals.

Glendurgan continues to introduce plants from across the world. Early scarlet *Rhododendron barbatum*, spruce, *Osmanthus* and *Pinus bhutanica* reflect the drama of Bhutan, their planting inspired by trips to the Himalayas made by Fox in the 1980s and by John Sales, chief gardens adviser to the National Trust, in the 1990s. On a 2012 visit to the Drakensberg Mountains in South Africa, gardener Ned Lomax (now at Bodnant, see pp. 46–51) acquired striking-looking heathers, *Erica discolor* and *E. verticillata*, which relish the similarly mild, wet climate of Glendurgan's valleys.

Any changes are made with an eye on the past; newly planted ornamental cherries among moisture-loving rodgersias, Japanese *Iris ensata* and spring snowflake *Leucojum vernum* in the Cherry Orchard recall when this boggy area was the original vegetable garden, planted with productive trees. The upturned Boat Seat refers to Fox's habit of keeping his gardening tools under a boat – a neat link with the garden's founder.

A delicate equilibrium has been reached in this lush valley. Exotic trees and shrubs flourish among native planting to create a distinctive and beautiful collection.

Holehird Gardens, Cumbria

At the heart of Holehird's gardens is a former walled kitchen garden with luxuriant borders and island beds. Beyond, bands of trees, shrubs and perennials curve up a hillside above Lake Windermere. And then there is the view from the Lower Garden to the interlocking mountains of Langdale Pikes, rising to over 2,600 feet. Holehird is on a mission to show what grows well in Lakeland gardens. Most plants are labelled, and several National Collections have been assembled within its 10 acres. If that sounds dry and daunting, fear not – its message is delivered with a light touch.

Holehird is gardened by the Lakeland Horticultural Society on land leased from the Holehird Trust, owners of the Victorian mansion below. Let until late 2021 as a care home, the house is separate from the gardens, but provides an extra dimension. Visible features that hint at the property's heyday include the 1871 kitchen garden walls, a stone staircase leading to a fountain on the Lower Terrace along which Victorian visitors would have strolled, and a former pit house, now a tufa house of alpines.

Less obvious is leaking Victorian pipework running beneath the gardens and carrying water from a spring that rises on the sheep-grazed hillside to reappear, first in the Walled Garden and then in the Gunnera Pool and Cascade of the Lower Garden, before eventually being piped into Lake Windermere via the Holehird Tarn.

Other features that tell of a grand Victorian garden include greenhouses, rhododendrons, a rockery, woodland and rose gardens – all of which have been reinterpreted for today. These elements tie in well together and the gardens beguile at any time of the year (they are always open).

Given Holehird is maintained entirely by volunteers with no overall head gardener, its coherence is surprising. Volunteers come when they please, and include a couple from southern England who garden at Holehird during regular holidays in the Lake District. The society's chair, Maggie Mees, looks after the bog garden of candelabra primulas, two early 20th-century ferns (*Osmunda regalis* 'Cristata'), gunnera and flag irises. 'Plans for tree planting or major design projects are presented for approval to the

Left Grass paths snake between beds that host a range of heathers and Holehird's National Collection of *Daboecia*.

Below An armillary sphere rests on a slate pedestal in the Walled Garden's lawn. Swirling round it are island beds, maintained collectively by a small group of volunteers. Late summer planting includes dahlias, physostegia, helianthus and symphyotrichum. The main tree is red-berried *Cotoneaster frigidus*.

Opposite Outcrops of Silurian sandstone make the slopes of the garden an ideal place for the Rock Garden. The stone is studded with alpines, including hebes, saxifrage, low-growing hardy geraniums, iris, gentians, pulsatillas, helianthemums, primulas and peonies.

An early area developed was the daffodil meadow, planted appropriately for a Windermere garden with Wordsworth's *Narcissus pseudonarcissus.*

garden committee,' says Maggie, 'but otherwise volunteers take ownership of the areas for which they are responsible.'

The uniting factor is the volunteers' response to the place. For example, there are no straight lines, as all the beds follow the land's contours, while the only plants grown are those suitable for the mostly acidic soil of the Lake District. Plants sold at Holehird's nursery have been propagated from the garden, so visitors can be confident that what they are buying will work in similar conditions.

An early area developed was the daffodil meadow, planted appropriately for a Windermere garden with Wordsworth's *Narcissus pseudonarcissus*. The volunteers then grouped together pines, heathers and alpines in families that mimic not just the Lakeland scenery but that of north-west China and Tibet, from which many plants came in the early 20th century.

Rhododendrons are planted above the Walled Garden in a glowing bank of pinks, oranges and yellows in May. Further round the hillside is the Rock Garden, a tapestry of acers, ericas, hypericums, dieramas and various pines, including *Chamaecyparis pisifera* 'Nana'. An ancient oak overshadows the Victorian Rock Pool, an original feature re-discovered in the 1980s by a gardener falling in. Skunk cabbage, water buttercups and bronze-tinged rodgersias grow in a spot also suitable for Holehird's National Collection of the mainly evergreen and hardy *Polystichum* ferns.

Other National Collections include the pink-flowered heather, *Daboecia*, and *Meconopsis*, the blue Himalayan poppy, which is completely happy growing in the Lakeland. The National Collection of Astilbes came to Holehird from Harewood House in 1987. Subtle differences (pink, red and white flowers, and green, dark green and almost purple stems) become apparent when astilbes are planted en masse.

Holehird also proves that shrub, climber, rugosa, pimpinellifolia and floribunda roses flourish in the Lakes, grown here with perennials in borders and island beds. Ornamental grasses, such as *Stipa gigantea*, *Miscanthus sinensis* 'Little Zebra' and *Calamagrostis* × *acutiflora* 'Overdam', are interwoven elsewhere with astrantia, dark contorted hazel, santolina and the starry white flowers of *Gillenia trifoliata*.

Within the Walled Garden, each wall-backed bed is planted according to aspect: bergenias, astrantias, sarcococcas and pulmonarias happier in the shade of the north-facing bed, and compact plantings of cannas, geums, phlox and dahlias in the sunnier beds that look west. Raised herb beds are designed for visitors in wheelchairs, as are newly laid paths across the hillside.

Holehird teaches stealthily, but above all enchants from the first snowdrops, hellebores, edgeworthias and pulmonarias in the Winter Border through to the glorious autumn display of grasses, hydrangeas, acers and the trees in the Woodland Walk.

Lamorran Gardens, Cornwall

At Lamorran Gardens, you plunge into an ocean of green. Owners Robert and Maria-Antonietta Dudley-Cooke have taken advantage of the borderline Mediterranean climate in their garden's south-west position overlooking the St Mawes estuary, and combined sub-tropical,

Above This palm-surrounded Ionic temple, with a wrought-iron dome, was inspired by a garden near Ventimiglia in Italy. Overlooking St Anthony's Head, it is a romantic setting for summer weddings.

oriental and Mediterranean influences in a paradise of sharply contemporary style. Chinese windmill palms (*Trachycarpus fortunei*) rise above a stone Italian balustrade, below which a Japanese gravel garden is framed by skimmia hedges. You quickly grasp that many different cultures have inspired this complex hillside garden.

When Robert and Maria-Antonietta moved to St Mawes in 1981, they found an overgrown small garden and a tennis court beside the house. The couple have since doubled the garden's size

to 4 acres, while the tennis court is now a rock-surrounded pool. The 300-foot drop from top to bottom allows mild air to push up and warm the planting.

Twisting gravel paths, steps, wooden walkways and stone bridges designed by Robert criss-cross the garden. Water streams down the hill, tripping over stone-edged pools that evoke the fountains of Rome, Maria-Antonietta's former home. Within the network of paths and streams, Robert planted shrubs, trees and succulents, but few herbaceous perennials. There is only one small lawn, surrounded by an amphitheatre of palms, with a central butia palm from South America. Azalea hedges on the upper levels are fiercely pruned to boost spring flower production.

Water streams down the hill, tripping over stone-edged pools that evoke the fountains of Rome, Maria-Antonietta's former home.

Keynote plants are palms and tree ferns, including dicksonias and tender *Cyathea cooperi*. Among the 200 palms are some of the biggest *Phoenix* palms on the UK mainland (only Tresco in the Isles of Scilly boasts bigger ones). A tender *Yucca elephantipes*, originally bought as a 3-foot plant from Marks & Spencer, is now a UK

Opposite An urn-topped lion fountain is the focal point of parallel lines of marble columns and classically inspired statues. This is one of many theatrical set-pieces that are so much a feature of Lamorran.

Right Tender blue bamboo (*Himalayacalamus hookerianus*) towers above a narrow cascade dropping down through the hillside. Acers and the trunks of *Schefflera taiwaniana* are underplanted with evergreen azaleas, an important element of Lamorran.

Below right A statue of Cleopatra emerges from a pool near the bottom of the garden, flanked by steps. Three further statues recall Maria-Antonietta's Italian homeland, while broken stone walls create a patina of age.

champion. A huge weeping birch is one of few original trees. Robert and Maria-Antonietta's introductions include a 50-foot *Pinus radiata* (grown from a 2-foot seedling), magnolias, yellow-flowered acacias, eucalyptus, the Chilean myrtle (*Luma apiculata*) with peeling orange bark, and its spring-flowering cousin, *Amomyrtus luma*.

Columns, statuary and a lion fountain contribute to an Italianate feel. Robert installed the first of two temples in 1997: weddings are held looking out towards St Anthony's Head in the one capped by an iron cupola. The cupola and its curtain of star jasmine *Trachelospermum jasminoides* with its scented white flowers were inspired by the garden at La Mortola on the Italian Riviera.

Ponds on every level attract damselflies, dragonflies, newts, tadpoles and mallard ducks. Descending past stands of rich purple and of green bamboo, you spot the estuary through pines, palms and tree ferns. Rhododendrons flourish, as do camellias and blue hydrangeas,

while on a sunny bank a South African bed is planted with proteas and leucospermum alongside spiky agaves, aeoniums and other succulents. South African protea *Leucadendron argenteum*, with its silvery foliage that glistens in sunshine, can be successfully grown in the mild far south-west of Britain and Isles of Scilly.

Over his years at Lamorran, Robert has noticed the effects of climate change, particularly with the palms, 50 of which once struggled to establish themselves. 'We haven't had a frost since 1987,' he says, 'so everything grows for 12 months of the year. Where I was once pushing the boundaries of possibilities with some plants, they are now bedding in happily.' Pelargoniums can be left out over the winter, as can tender, late-flowering, velvety tibouchina, and the bottlebrush plant (*Callistemon*) now has a second, late flush of flowers. Robert is also trialling a Kentia palm (*Howea forsteriana*), usually a houseplant in the UK. So content are the trachycarpus that they have seeded themselves in the garden, along the verge and into a field opposite.

Given these favourable conditions, one of the main challenges facing head gardener Jacob Howard-Endean is to keep things in shape and size when pruning but without losing their essence. Another recent task has been the opening up of a grove where rhododendrons that outlived their natural life have been replaced with further tree ferns, palms and bamboo. 'Gardening here is a continual process,' comments Jacob.

Above Wherever you are at Lamorran, you are conscious of the estuary beyond. Here, the view is outlined by palm trees (*Chamaerops humilis, Trachycarpus fortunei* and in the centre *Trithrinax acanthocoma*).

Overbeck's Garden, Devon

The best way to arrive at Overbeck's Garden in Devon is to take a 10-minute ferry from Salcombe and then transfer to the sea tractor that takes you up South Sands Beach. From there, a narrow track circles up the wooded cliffs to the tropical paradise of Overbeck's. The climb is worth it just for the view between towering pines and Chusan palms across the Salcombe Estuary to Prawle Point.

The garden was carved out of terraces connected by gravel paths and stone steps. Retaining walls, constructed of mica schist hewn from the headland's southern tip, have stood the test of time, their angularity hinting at the wild mountainous regions where much of the planting originated.

The palms, over 150 in total, are the signature of Overbeck's, which an inspired plantsman, Edric Hopkins, began planting in 1895. He saw that the precipitous 3.5-acre site would lend itself to the creation of a sub-tropical garden, and started introducing camphor trees, natives of the Malaysian jungle. This set the style of a garden, subsequently named for Otto Overbeck, a British-born inventor of Dutch descent, who lived here from 1928 to 1937, and bequeathed the property to the National Trust.

Hopkins' taste for exotics has been honoured for more than 120 years. The temperature here seldom drops below freezing in even the coldest winter. 'Once every ten years or so we have a frost that kills things off,' says head gardener

lilies (*Hedychium*), collected by plant hunter and former Wakehurst curator Tony Schilling. They were still scarce when brought here from the Royal Botanic Gardens, Kew in the 1980s to test their hardiness.

Palms run like hairy exclamation marks through near impenetrable planting below the wide terrace.

Spring comes early to this sheltered spot, signalled by magnificent magnolias. The deep pink Chinese *Magnolia campbellii* 'Overbecks' was planted by Edric Hopkins in 1901, and probably bought from pioneering Veitch Nurseries in Exeter, as was the pinky-white *Magnolia × veitchii*, bred by Peter Veitch in 1907. The *Magnolia campbellii*, coated in Spanish moss, fell onto its side in 1999, but after its crown was reduced, the phoenix put on new shoots and still dominates the Banana Garden.

Chris Groves. 'We then experiment and it keeps the garden refreshed.' There are pockets of acid and alkali, but most of the soil, says Chris, 'is fairly neutral and forgiving. It's been a conscious decision to choose unfamiliar plants to create a point of difference.'

Surrounding native woodlands contrast noticeably with Overbeck's, showing what a miracle the garden is. Several continents converge here – Mediterranean-style upper terraces with sea views and enclosed jungle areas lower down. Palms run like hairy exclamation marks through near impenetrable planting below the wide terrace. Other tropical plants include bananas, tree ferns and over a dozen varieties of ginger

Left The Banana Garden is a lush area where bananas don't need winter protection. Companion planting features *Fatsia japonica*, palmate-leafed *Tetrapanax papyrifer*, *Crinum* x *powellii* and *Canna indica* 'Purpurea'.

Below Cannas, knautias, bronze fennel and the bright flowers and strappy leaves of *Crocosmia* 'Lucifer' add depth and texture to the Statue Garden beds.

Opposite Chusan palms, echiums and pines frame the magnificent view over the Salcombe estuary. Other planting includes callistemon, blue agapanthus, feathery restios (*Cannomois grandis*), *Neopanax laetus* and silvery *Lavandula pinnata*.

Both Chile and Japan are represented on the Gazebo Garden's banks. Beneath graceful Chilean *Luma apiculata* are self-seeded roundels of this evergreen shrub from the myrtle family. These smaller specimens have been clipped into interlocking and undulating forms in a similar technique used for azaleas in Japan. Hardy down to -10°C, *L. apiculata* is a resilient substitute for box, although it needs clipping three to four times a year rather than once or twice.

Encircled by palms, the Statue Garden is a more conventional flower garden that transforms through the seasons. Tulips and *Gladiolus byzantinus* in spring are followed by a rich-plum, opium poppy, *Papaver somniferum* 'Lauren's Grape'. Primary-coloured dahlias, crocosmias, cannas, coreopsis and kniphofias predominate later in the year, accented with blue and purple salvias, agapanthus, *Geranium* 'Rozanne' and *Verbena bonariensis*. Nothing is taken out for over-wintering: dahlias and cannas take their chance. *First Flight*, a bronze statue of a young girl by sculptor Albert Bruce-Joy

(1842–1924) forms the centrepiece to the Statue Garden.

A box-blight-devastated parterre has been replaced by a chequerboard of mind-your-own-business (*Soleirolia soleirolii*), myrtle hedging and gravel. This fits well with the gravel-mulched Mediterranean planting on the upper terraces and around the lawn near the house. The silver foliage of olives is a highlight, along with *Stachys byzantina*, aromatic lavender, the European fan palm (*Chamaerops humilis*) and that Devon coastal staple, towering *Echium pininana*, originating from the Canary Islands but equally at home in the warm coastal climes of the South West. South African plants include grass-like restios and a curious, thistly stemmed member of the aster family, *Berkheya purpurea*, with mauve, flat flowers that resemble loudspeakers.

Your entry to Overbeck's down grand, palm-lined steps to the house terrace below is the perfect scene-setter to this garden wonderland, where different climate zones harmoniously co-exist and a sense of the exotic is enticingly within your grasp.

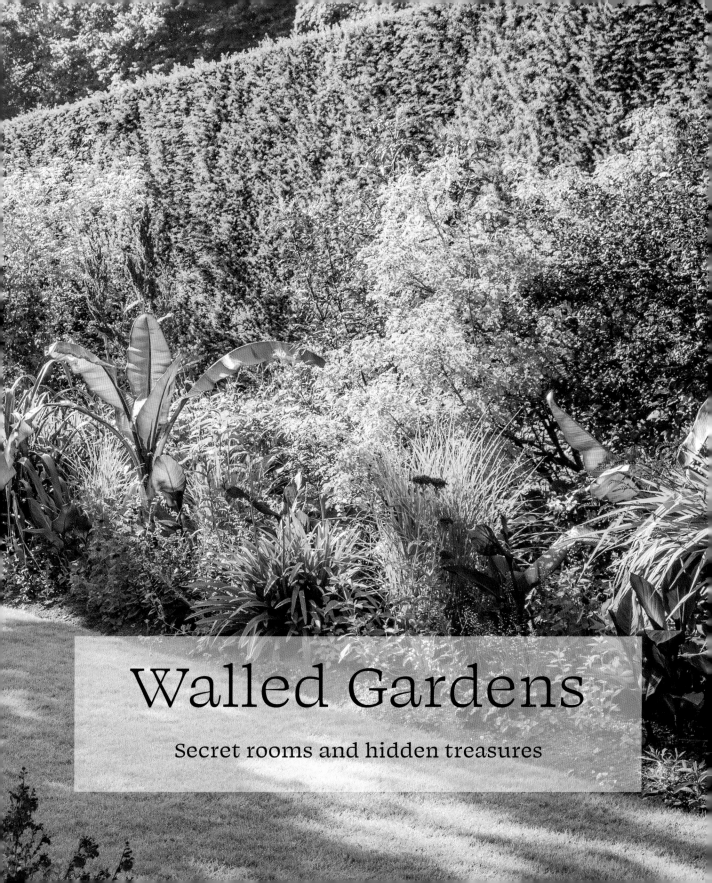

Walled Gardens

Secret rooms and hidden treasures

Previous page At Hidcote in Gloucestershire, the Red Borders peak in late summer with scarlet dahlias, salvias, cannas and lobelias, punctuated by dark elder (*Sambucus nigra*), berberis and *Cotinus coggygria* 'Royal Purple'. For contrast, there are grasses, dark-leafed phormiums, red bananas and *Pinus mugo*.

Opposite An aerial view of the kitchen garden quarter of the 4-acre site, conventionally and intensively planted with vegetables, herbs and fruit that supply the restaurant. The dovecote dates from the 1750s. In front of the conservatories are the Jewel Borders.

Felbrigg Hall, Norfolk

North-easterly sea winds whip across north Norfolk, yet Felbrigg Hall's 4-acre walled garden is indifferent. When head gardener Tina Hammond arrived in 1999, she realised that the garden was suitable for the type of planting she was already familiar with from four and a half years at Saltram in Devon.

Here you can expect to see both sub-tropical and arid planting. 'The red brick walls keep the garden like south-west England,' explains Tina. 'Yet thanks to Felbrigg being little more than a mile from the sea, it's cooler in summer. It extends the range of what we can plant.' Feature plants include chamaerops from North Africa and the Mediterranean; *Poncirus trifoliata*, a spiny citrus native to China and Korea; and puya, butia and the spiky *Colletia armata* from South America, the latter described by Tina as having 'wonderfully scented flowers that the bees love in late summer'.

Felbrigg was owned for over four centuries from the 1440s by the Wyndham family and is a 1,760-acre estate, complete with ice house, lake and ancient woodlands. The house has a grandly symmetrical Jacobean south front, with the west wing added during the Restoration and an early 18th-century orangery housing a camellia collection. The shelter belt, planted in the 1670s and 1680s, protects both house and garden. Its planter, William Windham I, was particularly fond of sweet chestnuts, but, according to a note written by him in 1676, 'I did then plant 4000 Oakes, 800 Ashes, 600 Birches, 70 Beeches, and 50 Crabs'.

Felbrigg was sold in 1863 to John Ketton, a Norwich merchant, who created the American Garden, planting Ohio buckeye (*Aesculus glabra*), Wellingtonia and western red cedars. Single-stemmed aralias, with huge pinnate leaves, are now being grouped to make a low-level canopy linking the orangery to the woodlands. A tetrapanax grove and an evergreen grove, including *Luma apiculata* and *Fatsia polycarpa*, with large, deeply toothed leaves (more commonly seen in south-west England), have also been planted.

The walled garden has attracted the lion's share of attention since the National Trust took over in 1969. Researching its history, Tina has

found receipts for bricks delivered to Felbrigg from the 1750s, showing that the walls and octagonal dovecote, with 2,000 nesting boxes still in use, date from that decade.

The central circular stone pond was added in the 1840s, along with the cross-wall topped by pinecone finials. Seventeenth-century stonework from the house was used for a doorway in the south wall – and other arches in the walls give views across the garden.

Ted Bulloch, the first head gardener appointed by the Trust, cleared wall-to-wall brambles and a quarter acre of horseradish before planting box hedging and reseeding lawns. In Tina's time, the garden has been further transformed, with its history and contemporary planting pleasingly balanced. The garden is divided into four, a quarter being a traditional kitchen garden that supplies the restaurant and intermingles ornamental planting with herbs and vegetables. Reminders of its past are apricots, pears, cherries,

nectarines, plums and 'Norfolk Beefing', a culinary apple dating from the 16th century, trained along the walls. Many were replanted by Ted in the 1970s – but there are still some 18th-century fig trees, carefully pruned in February.

In the Nuttery, hazels grow informally with woodland planting and fruit trees. In the other two quarters, walled-garden convention has been thrown to the wind, as in the Treasure Garden, where the double Jewel Borders are punctuated by cordylines and tall lilies. From beneath them, orange marigolds, cerise lychnis and purple-headed *Allium sphaerocephalon* spill out across gravel paths.

Stony paths wind through the drought-tolerant borders, which feature plants uncommon in north Norfolk.

The Bacchus Garden evokes hotter climes. Stony paths wind through the drought-tolerant borders, which feature plants uncommon in north Norfolk. These include agaves, leptospermums and *Dasylirion acrotrichum*, a bristly succulent with a palm-like trunk native to Mexican deserts. An olive grove, pruned into goblets, summons up the Mediterranean, with

Above Beside one of the old conservatories in the Treasure Garden are the Jewel Borders. Herbaceous perennials are blended with *Stipa gigantea* and *Trachycarpus fortunei* that prosper in the micro-climate just inland from the coast.

Right In the Bacchus Garden, palms (*Washingtonia robusta*) and grasses grow with osteospermums, pelargoniums and *Erigeron karvinskianus*.

fig and grape motifs decorating a galvanised gazebo and wrought-iron benches crafted by a local blacksmith.

Introducing different styles of planting, and building up the borders have made Felbrigg high maintenance. This doesn't worry Tina Hammond. 'We have a fabulous team of dedicated volunteers. And I've had the freedom to do so much.'

Hidcote, Gloucestershire

Set on the Cotswold escarpment, Hidcote's green rooms within walls of yew, box, beech and holly offer surprise after surprise. The garden was created by Major Lawrence Johnston, a British-naturalised American who settled in Gloucestershire in 1907. He matched hedging with Cotswold stone, red brick and fine detailing in an inspired adaptation of Arts and Crafts principles. The movement's reaction against mass production was exemplified in gardens by a rejection of hot-housed carpet bedding and by the use of vernacular stone.

Johnston faced many tests across his 10.5 acres, not the least being its elevation 600 feet above sea level, land sloping awkwardly away from the small Cotswold manor and a huge cedar of Lebanon by the house. The cedar became his starting point: he sowed a lawn around it and created a central corridor past hedges, walls and gates and through the Red Borders and the pleached hornbeams of the Stilt Garden. He loved yew, not only for hedging but also clipped into roundels, pyramids and even into a pedimented arch by the Bathing Pool.

The influence of European gardens is also visible in Hidcote's terracing and its two main vistas: the hedged Italianate Long Walk and the main axis, which rise up to wrought-iron gates opening onto views of the Cotswold and Malvern Hills.

Colour-themed gardens were laid out around the house, threaded through by paths of Cotswold stone and red brick. Johnston alternated these planterly compartments with green courts, such as the yew-encircled Great Lawn, and with more open spaces around the periphery.

In 1948, Johnston handed Hidcote, unendowed, to the National Trust, which then had to maintain what had become a world-famous garden with limited resources. Lottie Allen, head gardener since 2019, believes that adaptations made by the Trust over the years lost something of Johnston's guiding spirit. In 2023, she saw the 75th anniversary of Hidcote's joining the Trust as an opportunity to review the garden. 'One source was *Country Life* articles written by Henry Avray Tipping illustrating how the garden looked in the 1930s and 40s,' she explains.

'Climate change and new pests and diseases don't allow exact replication of Johnston's planting, but we're trying to retrieve the original atmosphere.'

As Johnston intended, each garden will increasingly have its own season. The White Garden's simple palette of pure white phlox, veronicastrums and geraniums is now designed to peak in July and early August. The terrace above the Bathing Pool has been similarly streamlined for high summer with dark red snapdragons and fuchsias. In both, beds are edged by shiny *Euonymus japonicus* 'Microphyllus', being tested as an alternative to box.

Johnston allowed for divergences, so, says Lottie, 'borders that can take it are still densely planted'. The double Red Borders, bookended by brick gazebos, are at full throttle in August with cannas, dahlias, bright red salvias, hemerocallis and the stand-out spires of *Lobelia cardinalis* 'Queen Victoria'. These heady oranges and reds are offset by blue flashes of agapanthus and by the dark foliage of shrubs such as *Cotinus coggygria* and berberis. *Pinus mugo* and strappy grasses are green accents.

Johnston's colour schemes have always been honoured. The Old Garden has walls on three sides and tiered beds of mostly pastel planting. Hellebores, white fritillaries, scillas and pulmonaria are followed by geraniums, salvias, roses (including the semi-double yellow *Rosa* 'Lawrence Johnston' on one wall), peonies and silver-leafed phlomis. Sedums, big, blowsy purple dahlias and *Aster × frikartii* 'Mönch' complete the show in autumn.

A tapestry hedge of copper and green beech, holly and yew (in which the copper beech has won out) frames the Circle, a pivotal point on the central axis with a lawn encircled by brick paths, knee-high *Lavandula angustifolia* 'Munstead' and May-flowering lilac *Syringa × chinensis*. In Mrs Winthrop's Garden, designed as a warm spot for Johnston's elderly mother, the blue and yellow theme continues across the year. Coronillas, *Euphorbia characias* subsp. *wulfenii* and scillas are succeeded by *Alchemilla mollis*, tree peonies, agapanthus, aconitums

Above The Bathing Pool Garden is one of three circular gardens to the south of the manor house. Twice-blooming 'Iceberg' roses maintain floral interest across the summer, while a magnolia is underplanted with brunnera, *Delphinium* 'Faust' and cimicifuga.

Right The pleached hornbeams (*Carpinus betulus*) of the Stilt Garden above the Red Borders frame a wrought-iron gate that opens onto a view towards the Malvern Hills.

and creeping Jenny (*Lysimachia nummularia* 'Aurea').

In the Pillar Garden, yew columns stand in low wall beds of Cotswold stone and are half-submerged in late summer by pink roses, cleome, nemesia and *Salvia involucrata* clashing with

---

In the Pillar Garden, yew columns are half-submerged in late summer by pink roses, cleome, nemesia and salvia.

---

orange crocosmia and lilies. Pines, rock roses, cistus and sea hollies, ideal for increasingly dry summers, thrive in the Rock Bank, reminiscent of Serre de la Madone, Johnston's Mediterranean home near Menton in southern France.

On the dry Alpine Terrace, tender South African rhodohypoxis, *Berkheya purpurea* and *Erigeron karvinskianus* grow in south-facing, raised gravel beds. In the further reaches of the garden, such defined areas give way to more natural plantings in the damp Wilderness and Stream Gardens and the woodland Wilderness. You are never far from water at Hidcote: a stream bubbles past acers in the Maple Garden near the entrance and can be heard from the White Garden. It disappears underground to emerge near a white magnolia in the Upper Stream, running across stepping stones and jumping down low stone waterfalls past skunk cabbage, marsh marigolds and banks of ferns, before continuing beyond the gardens out into the Cotswold countryside.

Above Columns of yew run through the Pillar Garden, enfolded by a soft colour palette of campanulas, salvias, geraniums, diascia and lilies, with crocosmias as a bright accent.

Below right Over herb beds in the East Walled Garden, you can glimpse planting in the West Walled Garden through an archway in the early 19th-century brick walls. Many of the walls inside the garden are adorned with climbers and espaliers.

Llanerchaeron, Ceredigion

It's a beautiful drive across Wales to Llanerchaeron. Travelling westwards, you pass the conical peak of Sugar Loaf outside Abergavenny and the looming Bannau Brycheiniog (Brecon Beacons). Beyond Lampeter, valleys open out to the coastal plain where the River Aeron runs into the sea at Aberaeron. Two miles inland is the elegant Georgian villa of Llanerchaeron, with a lake, pleasure grounds of some 8 acres and two walled gardens burgeoning with a wealth of fruit, vegetables, herbs and flowers.

The house is a simple, cream-coloured, two-storey villa built between 1794 and 1796 by John Nash, architect of Regent Street, while in west Wales evading his London creditors. Llanerchaeron was once a self-contained estate owned by ten generations of the Lewis (later Lewes) family until it was bequeathed to the National Trust in 1989 by John Powell Ponsonby Lewes. Its brick and stone estate buildings survive, including the bailiff's house and the gardener's bothy, which abut the red brick walls of the kitchen garden. These walls absorb the

sun's heat and were built at the same time as Nash's villa. The clay was sourced on site from the fittingly named Cae Brics (Brick Field) during the making of the lake.

Contorted apple and pear trees, probably between 150 and 200 years old, have become like candelabras.

The East and West Walled Gardens between them cover just under 2 acres. Almost everything here is grown from seeds and cuttings, with the produce sold at reception and anything unfit for consumption composted; nothing is wasted. An area is set aside for runner beans, umbelliferous parsnips and the huge allium heads of leeks left to yield seed for the following year. 'Twelve kale plants,' says gardener Megan Hall, 'provide enough seed for years.' Green manure (phacelia and field beans) is sown on empty beds while, experimentally, grass cuttings are used as moisture-retaining mulch. 'We need to check the nutrient balance,' explains fellow gardener Alex Muir. 'Grass mulch might mean too much green leggy growth rather than flowers and fruit. We test out different things every year, particularly trying to avoid water evaporation in warm weather.'

Contorted apple and pear trees are probably between 150 and 200 years old. They would originally have been espaliers, but over the years, the upper horizontal branches have turned upright and become like candelabras.

Opposite The now completely dilapidated Welsh-made 1950s concrete greenhouse is a period piece that fascinates historians and visitors alike.

Right Much of the focus at Llanerchaeron is on productive gardening, but the herbaceous borders add another dimension to the scene. Here, the perennial planting includes phlox, hylotelephium and veronicastrum.

Below Over the last 150 years or more, espaliered apple and pear trees have grown out into elaborate candelabra. Llanerchaeron is gardened in a nature-conscious manner, without chemicals and with companion planting of marigolds to ward blackfly off brassicas.

Interspersed are newer espaliers of both apples and pears. Plums, greengages and other fruit trees have also been espaliered on south-facing walls within and outside the gardens.

There have been greenhouses here since the mid-1800s, but what remains are the brick footings of one with white walls to radiate heat for trained fruit. Sunflowers, tomatoes and French marigolds grow in a gap between two wooden greenhouses, where the heating pipes, benching and metal window struts and winding gear are still visible. A ruinous concrete greenhouse, made in Wales in the 1950s, is home to camellias and a vine – and out of bounds even to the gardening team.

Tradition sits comfortably with newer adaptations. A dipping pond in each of the gardens was once fed by springs on the estate and used for filling watering cans. One with

bulrushes is now girdled by yew hedging, the other by ferns, waterlilies, evening primroses and rodgersias that attract dragonflies and newts.

Wildflower meadows have been introduced where there were once old fruit bushes. These plats of grass are left long through the summer and already southern marsh, early purple and spotted orchids are appearing. To suppress the grass and encourage more wild flowers, yellow rattle seed from the wider estate will be sown.

In the East Garden, raised wooden beds, containing over 100 varieties of herbs, have been arranged on an earlier 'piano key'-style footprint. Bees hum round hyssop, germander, sorrel, angelica, Fuller's teasel (once used for carding wool), camomile and woad for dyeing. There are fruit cages of redcurrants and raspberries, with globe and Jerusalem artichokes and many varieties of rhubarb beside one wall. On other walls, annuals are blended with perennials (cosmos and meadowsweet with sedums, ligularia, phlox and hemerocallis), and camellias are repeated through brunnera, heuchera, astrantia, persicaria and crocosmia.

The sympathy of the gardening team and volunteers for the old ways helps preserve this beautifully tranquil and unique garden. This care extends beyond the walls to the management of the lake and of the parkland, which is carpeted with flowers in spring.

Scampston, North Yorkshire

Scampston Hall in North Yorkshire has a fine pedigree. Its domed Regency house features a 'Capability' Brown landscape designed in the late 1770s. Characteristically, it has a lawn merged with parkland over a ha-ha, lakes, cascade and an elegant Palladian bridge. You can wander the parkland's 80 acres along fine meandering trails, but since 2004 Scampston's chief attraction has been the Walled Garden.

The 4.5-acre kitchen garden had been derelict for 50 years before it was taken in hand in 1999 by Sir Charles and Lady Legard, whose family have owned Scampston since 1690. Audaciously, they commissioned a contemporary garden from Dutch designer Piet Oudolf.

A pioneer of the New Perennial movement, Oudolf has pulled off quite a trick. On entering, you follow a path between beech hedging and pleached limes with shrub borders behind. Turn

Above The Perennial Meadow demonstrates Piet Oudolf's distinctive style, featuring perennials used in great blocks of colour for maximum impact. Planting here includes phlomis, hardy geraniums and *Salvia nemorosa* 'Amethyst'.

Above Drifts of Grass is the visitor's introduction to this unconventional walled garden. Sinuous bands of *Molinia* 'Poul Petersen' weave through mown grass towards a grove of four *Phellodendron chinensis*.

Left Alliums and *Phlomis russeliana* edge the red brick paths that run through the Perennial Meadow and much of the Walled Garden.

the corner and you are kept waiting by another allée, more hedging and borders of annuals, perennials, grasses and shrubs beneath a rosy-leafed *Cercis canadensis* 'Forest Pansy', acers and a fastigiate liquidambar. Only after you have turned yet another corner does Oudolf's main design finally disclose itself in garden rooms mostly as naturalistic as Brown's parkland.

You are faced first by the Drifts of Grass: swathes of *Molinia* 'Poul Petersen' snaking through closely mown grass. Oudolf plays with form everywhere. In the Silent Garden, he has planted 24 10-foot-high columns of yew in

Oudolf's ethos is that plants should grow, live and die gracefully, so seedheads are left on and nothing is staked.

plinths around a dark, off-centre pool. Two Box Gardens each contain 10-foot squares of box topped with a pimple. In the Spring Box Garden are narrow borders of grasses and perennials against beech hedging, while the Summer Box Garden's borders are wider and stronger in colour: more grasses, but also eupatoriums,

salvias, tall yellow achilleas, monardas, heleniums and dark origanum.

Most surprising is the juxtaposition of the Perennial Meadow and the 1894 conservatory. Yew runs through horseshoe-shaped beds of naturalised planting, with the form of every plant, seed and flower head equally important. Around red-brick seating areas plantings include nepeta, salvia and knautia and grasses, more redolent of prairies rather than kitchen gardens. Oudolf's ethos is that plants should grow, live and die gracefully, so seedheads are left on and nothing is staked.

Yew groynes and roundels within compartments of beech surround the Katsura

Grove of caramel-scented *Cercidiphyllum japonicum*. The trees are underplanted with grasses, including *Molinia* 'Transparent', acanthus, persicaria and dainty white-flowered *Gillenia trifoliata*. Oudolf nods at the garden's original use with a Potager and a Cut Flower Garden in which 12 circular beds among fruit trees are heaped with sweet peas, umbellifers, cleome, grasses, nigella and salvias. Huge sunflowers are planted with *Nicotiana* 'Lime Green' and *Zinnia* 'Benary's Lime Green', and chocolate cosmos with 'Black Ball' cornflowers, dark red dahlias and amaranth.

Ad hoc replanting has occasionally strayed from Oudolf's intentions, says head gardener Andy Karavics. 'We are revitalising the design and removing some replacements,' he explains. He and his team are working through the Serpentine Garden where yew roundels and clover shapes are encircled by smallish trees such

as *Parrotia persica* and largish shrubs such as euonymus. Oudolf's concept is being restored by introducing more painted lady's ferns (*Athyrium niponicum* f. *metallicum*) that like the woodland habitat. A *Cornus kousa* is replacing a sweetgum. 'Liquidambar is a lovely tree,' says Andy, 'but will grow too big and out of proportion with Oudolf's design.'

For the best view, climb the Mount above wildflower plats and cherry trees. From there you will see that Oudolf's approach, though startling within the walls of a former kitchen garden, perfectly complements Brown's parkland outside.

Wallington, Northumberland

If you approach Wallington via a narrow Palladian bridge over the River Wansbeck, you are struck by the sight of Owl House, set high up against trees. Bridge and building were designed as a *mise en scène* in the mid-18th century: the Owl House as an eye-catcher from the bridge but also as a viewing pavilion over the 20-square-mile Wallington estate.

The red brick Owl House gets its name from the stone owl (as represented on the Calverley family crest) sitting atop its roof. It dominates the spectacular 1760s Walled Garden that lies 15 minutes' walk from the grey Palladian mansion. The house was remodelled in the 1740s for Sir Walter Calverley Blackett and is reached via a 1754 Clock Tower, with a Doric cupola. Despite this grandeur, the atmosphere is laid-back: children play and adults relax in deckchairs on lawns around the house and in a grass courtyard, heavy with lime scent in mid-summer. The informal woodlands laid out in the 1730s may have influenced 'Capability' Brown, who was born in 1716 at nearby Kirkharle.

But what of the secluded Walled Garden? The route here lies through these woodlands, past a fallen oak, one of 15,000 trees uprooted by Storm Arwen in November 2021. As a stark reminder, the oak's root plate has been left exposed, unmoved from the spot where it fell, and images of weather carved into its trunk.

Unlike in a traditional kitchen garden, the 4-acre Walled Garden has no straight lines:

Left A long stretch of greenhouses on the top terrace of the Walled Garden is fronted by the dazzling Hot Border, a brash mixture of *Dahlia* 'Fire Mountain', grasses *Stipa tenuissima* and *Uncinia rubra*, cannas and *Potentilla thurberi* 'Monarch's Velvet'.

Opposite Curving stone steps encircle Lady Mary's Pool, planted with clumps of bergenia. Beside the steps are dark blue *Salvia nemorosa* 'Caradonna', silver *Eryngium bourgatii*, *Mahonia* x *media* 'Charity' and pale lilac *Allium cernuum*.

The garden's many different rooms and terraces are encircled by walls and hedges, cut through by gravel, stone and brick paths.

The Walled Garden was run down when the National Trust took over Wallington in 1958. The then gardens advisor, Graham Stuart Thomas, made the garden entirely ornamental for more visitor interest and to be less labour-intensive than vegetable gardening. His colour themes are still followed, although planting changes constantly. 'The advantage is that we are not stuck in one period,' says head gardener Simon Thompson, who has been at Wallington for nearly 25 years.

The Blue and Yellow Borders cut through the middle of the garden beneath honeysuckle arches underplanted by blue delphiniums, geraniums, nepeta and eryngiums, mixed with yellow loosestrife and hemerocallis. Composed mainly of annuals grown on site, the brash, hot border-planting on the Owl House terrace contrasts with the subtle gradations from darker to paler shades in the Pale Border. The Cut Flower Borders, retained within low dry-stone walls around a central lawn, feature multi-coloured

dog-legged in shape, it was wedged for its protection from wind into a former hawthorn dell and slopes in two directions. On one side, a red vine (*Vitis coignetiae*) rockets up into parkland trees; on the other, cows look down from fields directly above the walls. The crowns of the trees within the Walled Garden, including an *Acer* 'Crimson King', blur the boundaries by picking up the shapes of parkland trees beyond.

The estate's last owner, Sir Charles Trevelyan, and his wife, Mary, began gardening ornamentally here in the 1930s. Lady Mary's Pool was created in 1938, with a semi-circular balustrade outlined by box hedging and walls speckled with erigeron, ferns and alchemilla. Flanking steps curl round to the pool from which a rill runs down through the lawn below.

The brash, hot border planting on the Owl House terrace contrasts with the subtle gradations from darker to paler shades in the Pale Border.

annuals and perennials, supported by hazel cages and rising to 9 foot by late summer. Further down the garden, the Nuttery has blocks of wild flowers and beehives set within log fencing. A wall-backed border is packed with heleniums, bronze fennel, rodgersias, phlox, astrantias, salvia and perovskia with the smoke bush *Cotinus coggygria* 'Royal Purple' above.

Simon likes the diversity of species in the lawns where daisies, clover and moss pop up, while the middle lawn is planted with 100,000 purple crocuses for an eye-catching spring-time display. These open lawns are breathing spaces between tight enclosures of planting, the most recent of which is the Garden of Imagination, enclosed by yew and hornbeam, and conceived by Simon as a private area for storytelling. Quotations from William Blake are carved into the stone path round a big yew and oak throne, made by a volunteer on the estate. Dark-coloured, unusual-shaped perennials are mixed with shrubs, a contorted hazel and the silky red grass, *Hordeum jubatum*, to create a secluded retreat and a further moment of pause within this spectacular garden.

Opposite The 18th-century Owl House is visible from miles around. Framed by the dark foliage of an *Acer* 'Crimson King' is soft planting of geraniums and ferns, with *Hypericum olympicum*, *Viburnum henryi* and *Osmanthus burkwoodii*.

Right A brick path runs through the Blue and Yellow Border, which cuts across the centre of the Walled Garden. Honeysuckle arches are underplanted with blue nepeta, delphiniums, *Allium moly* and yellow loosestrife, hemerocallis and dominant *Centaurea macrocephala*.

Below Sheep graze in the fields above the Walled Garden. In the narrow bed in the foreground grow *Tanacetum coccineum*, phlox and lupins.

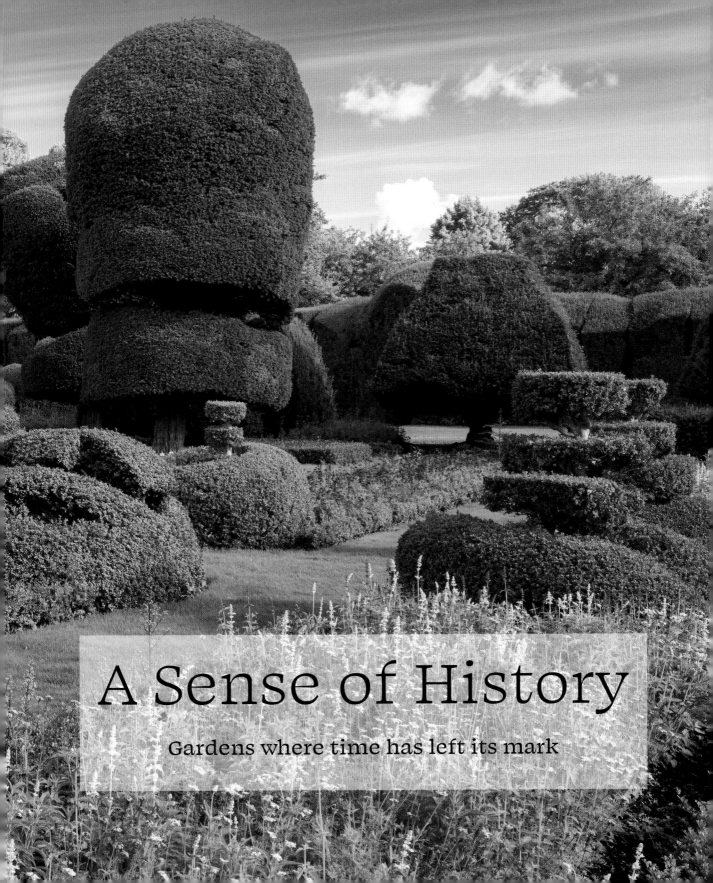

A Sense of History

Gardens where time has left its mark

Previous page Beneath the yews in the Topiary Garden at Levens Hall, Cumbria, is a tapestry of summer annual planting. Featured are creams (*Antirrhinum* 'Liberty Classic Yellow' and golden agastache); blues and purples (*Heliotropium* 'Marine', *Verbena* 'Imagination' and *Salvia farinacea* 'Rhea'); and pastel pinks (*Verbena* 'Serenity', *Salvia farinacea* 'White' and *Agastache* 'Rose Mint').

Opposite The view to the rugged peak of the Old Man of Coniston first attracted the Victorian sage to his home beside Coniston Water. *Rhododendron* 'Broughtonii' was planted by Ruskin's devoted cousin, Joan Severn.

Brantwood, Cumbria

John Ruskin, art critic and philosopher, was attracted to Brantwood by its seclusion, facing west over Coniston Water towards the Lake District's craggy peak, the Old Man of Coniston. He bought Brantwood in 1871 and lived there until his death in 1900, turning the country cottage into an Arts and Crafts house. For him, the 250-acre estate was a refuge, where, on moorland and fellside, he put into effect his naturalistic view of gardening in carefully contrived, thematic areas that aligned with the values of the Arts and Crafts movement. Ruskin was ahead of his time with his thoughts on rewilding.

Brantwood was Ruskin's outdoor laboratory, but there is more to its story. It is a garden of two distinct styles, and two physical parts, with the Lower Garden, running down to the private jetty, divided from house and hillside by a lane.

Ruskin was supported through bouts of mental illness by his cousin, Joan, wife of painter Arthur Severn. So important was Joan to Ruskin that he not only bequeathed her the estate, but even accepted her taste in gardening. His domain appears rough-hewn from the fells, while Joan's planting is a last hurrah of Victorian formalism. Visitors who arrived by boat would have entered Brantwood through the Lower Garden and Joan ensured they were greeted in style, stepping off the boat to follow a showy curving avenue – the width of her dresses – planted with azaleas, then interspersed with lilacs and an understorey of bedding plants. This walk has filled out with relaxed perennials, but the intention is to reinstate the lilacs and make the planting here and through the nearby Trellis Garden closer to the formality of Joan's day. Sally Beamish, head gardener from 1998 to 2014, did much to rescue Brantwood from near chaos and laid out the Trellis Garden in tribute to Joan. Joan's influence

> For Ruskin, the 250-acre estate was a refuge, where, on moorland and fellside, he put into effect his naturalistic view of gardening.

Above Terraced slopes, known as Zig-Zaggy, were inspired by Ruskin's observations of mountain farming in northern Italy and by Dante's *Inferno*. They are planted with phormiums and grasses and mulched with sheep's wool and charcoal, the latter symbolising Hell.

Left An *Acer palmatum* overhangs the Maple Walk that connects Ruskin's area of the garden with Joan Severn's High Walk.

is also felt in the Maple Walk and in the High Walk, where the forms of a double border of colourful azaleas and rhododendrons echo the mountainous ridge across the lake.

The rest of the estate is triumphantly the work of Ruskin's imagination. In the Lower Garden is Ruskin's daffodil field, including *Narcissus poeticus*, *N. pseudonarcissus* and other alpine cultivars he introduced. His Hortus Inclusus, the shape of its beds based on the dining room windows of the house, is to become a children's allotment, with a wormery and composting area, reflecting Ruskin's interest in education.

When Sally came to Brantwood in the 1990s, she uncovered stony pathways that wind upwards through Italianate terraces known as Zig-Zaggy, each section signifying a Seven Deadly Sin described in Dante's *Inferno*. Upside down and difficult to reach espaliered pears represent greed, while the wiry, evil-looking cotoneaster betokens anger. Sheep's wool is used as mulch, as is charcoal, its blackness symbolising Hell. At the top, you reach Paradise, where light plays through a mossy glade of hazel, birch and oak.

In the Professor's Garden, Ruskin grew ornamentals and edibles, based on what a labourer might have planted in a similarly sized allotment. According to Brantwood head gardener Simone Daye, they are now trying out the traditional companion-planting method of intercropping called 'Three Sisters', with runner

beans putting nitrogen into the soil and climbing up corn, while squash grow beneath, covering the ground and retaining moisture. 'This is true to Ruskin's vision of experimentation,' she says, 'but moving forward. We are also planting alliums to repel whitefly and nasturtiums as a sacrifice plant for aphid pest control.'

You keep climbing, eventually arriving at Ruskin's stone seat. It is set deliberately with its back to the lake so that he could focus on studying water tumbling from a beck. This filled a pool, made by Ruskin, who also designed the reservoirs and sluices that fed the house's water system. He stocked the pool with fish and spent

hours observing and drawing insects. There is always the unexpected: on one occasion, heavy rains washed the fish into Coniston Water.

Ruskin oversaw the placing of every locally quarried stone in the Precipice Steps that ascend through woods towards the moors. Part of the moorland was terraced for his experiments with what we now call permaculture. He tried and failed to grow wheat, but then was successful with apples. 'We now have 20 grafted apple trees to plant up in the Moorland Garden,' says Simone. Soft fruit bushes and cherries will be added further down the slopes.

Today, you still feel Ruskin is at hand, largely thanks to the reconstruction work of

Above Ruskin turned a small cottage into an imposing Arts and Crafts house, seen here through apple blossom. The orchard is in the Lower Garden, rescued from neglect by head gardener Sally Beamish in the early 2000s.

Sally Beamish. Brantwood is a green, engulfing garden, with a constant oscillation between the grand and the intimate. New plans are drawn up with Ruskin's principles in mind, but also to move the garden forward. This drive to test and improve is true to the essence of all his work.

Right Looking over the grey border towards the *Clematis viticella* obelisks in the pastel border. In the foreground are silver-leafed *Lychnis coronaria*, sea kale, nepeta, stachys and verbascum.

Levens Hall, Cumbria

The Topiary Garden at Levens Hall is the oldest and most extensive of its kind in the world, created by a French designer, Guillaume Beaumont, in 1694. Come the early 18th century, the English Landscape Movement rendered clipped evergreens and hedged enclosures obsolete. Many such gardens were ripped out and replanted in a naturalistic style to symbolise the difference between the British constitutional monarchy and the unbending autocracy of France. Levens, fortunately, survived.

The layout has changed little since the 1690s. Many of the 100 topiary forms date from Beaumont's time, clipped from yew, golden yew and various forms of box. They include chess pieces (the king and queen), a judge's wig, a lion, umbrellas, Queen Elizabeth I and her maids of honour, a jug and four peacocks. Growing up some topiary pieces and encircling yew hedging is the Scottish flame flower, *Tropaeolum speciosum*, a splash of red against dark green.

Box-edged beds are planted out with 15,000 home-grown annuals resembling embroidery with four main colours: yellow, dark blue, light

The layout has changed little since the 1690s. Many of the 100 topiary forms date from Beaumont's time, clipped from yew, golden yew and various forms of box.

Left Borage and marigolds, chosen to attract bees and other pollinators, flower in the Bee Borders. The Borders are sown with an annual seed mix called Medieval Carpet (available from Marshalls Seeds).

Below The parallel Bee Borders run through the Orchard, where the old fruit trees are valued as much for their blossom in spring as for their autumn harvest. They include apples, pears, medlars, quinces and damsons.

Opposite Changes are rung annually in the beds of the Topiary Garden. In the central bed is a higher growing mix of cleome, cosmos and *Verbena bonariensis*. In the background is Beaumont's House, the head gardener's home.

blue and pastel pink. Daisies and pansies are followed in summer by *Salvia* 'Fairy Queen', *Lavandula multifida*, heliotrope, verbenas, cleome and golden agastache. 'There are blocks of colour, but the planting is soft and natural-looking, contrasting with the yew's formality,' says head gardener Chris Crowder.

Near the Rose Garden, planted mainly with pink, crimson and white David Austin roses, is Beaumont's House. This is home to Chris, who came to Levens in 1986, only the tenth head gardener in over 300 years. 'I am very respectful of Levens's history,' he explains. 'This garden has evolved down the centuries, and because the estate has remained in family ownership for 700 years, I'm not weighed down by committees.'

The Topiary Garden that everyone associates with Levens is not the only survivor of Guillaume Beaumont's design: also extant are the Bowling Green, now a croquet lawn, and the beech hedges that run through the garden's centre. In the Wilderness, some old lime trees and a pedimented alcove remain of former pleasure grounds that featured shady walks and shrubberies. Paths are cut through longer grass, which is strimmed in July.

By the Bowling Green are the double Pastel Borders, with pyramids of clematis giving

Above Vegetables are planted in narrow borders, backed on two sides by yew hedging. Rhubarb is planted down the shadier pathway between the yew hedges, with the feathery tops of asparagus by the beech arch.

rhythm to mid-summer herbaceous planting of frothy white *Crambe cordifolia*, the giant yellow scabious (*Cephalaria gigantea*) and fluffy meadow rue (*Thalictrum flavum*), with foliage contrast from *Hosta sieboldiana* var. *elegans*. 'I am keen,' says Chris, 'that the garden should give a different visual hit in each area.' In the Fountain Garden's Red Border, late summer impact comes from the rugosa rose, 'Roseraie de l'Haÿ', and the dark foliage of *Dahlia* 'Bishop of Llandaff', cannas, atriplex and persicaria interspersed with silver willow.

Through the Orchard of ancient apples, medlars, quinces, pears and damsons, many wreathed in mistletoe, run the Bee Borders. These are sown with borage, marigolds, echiums and mallows to attract bees and provide a long season of colour.

Highly decorative vegetable borders supply Levens's restaurant. 'They are very productive,' says Chris, 'but we are also very conscious of how

they look.' This area repeats the pattern found in other sections of the garden – a circle and four crossing paths. Vegetables are selected for colour, texture and form, with red and yellow chard stems, bull's blood beetroot and feathery carrot tops, plus onions, fennel and lettuce. Many of the vegetable plants (beans, courgettes, asparagus) remain to give shape and interest beyond harvest. A final cruciform garden is planted with herbs, the layout recalling the structure of the great Topiary Garden where your visit began. It is the majestic presence of this topiary that informs the whole garden and the vision of Levens that will linger long in your memory.

Mount Stewart, County Down

On a sunny morning, Mount Stewart is irresistibly lovely. As you approach the gardens along its shores, the waters of sheltered Strangford Lough sparkle like the Mediterranean. It seems only appropriate that the gardens feature both a terraced Italian Garden and a Spanish

Above The magnolia-clad south front of Mount Stewart house forms an imposing backdrop to the richly planted Italian Garden. Beds lined with low hedges of berberis, dwarf rhododendrons and potentilla overflow in late summer with an exuberant mix of cannas, lychnis, helianthus and eupatorium, while standard trained glory bushes, crepe myrtle and giant dahlias add height to the display.

Garden; the green-tiled roof of the summerhouse recalling the Generalife in Granada.

The grey stone house is mostly early 19th century, when the 3rd Marquess of Londonderry built the stately entrance, the hall with its dome and flanking columns, grand drawing room and dining room.

The grandeur is matched outside. The formal terracing and themed plantings were planned in the 1920s and 1930s by Edith, wife of the 7th Marquess of Londonderry. The couple came to live here when the marquess was Minister of Education in the Ulster Parliament from 1921 to 1926. They turned Mount Stewart

into a family home, as it remains today with their granddaughter, Lady Rose Lauritzen, still living there. To give the mansion the setting it originally lacked, Lady Londonderry made sweeping changes using the large workforce available after First World War demobilisation. The garden's position in a warm recess between Strangford and Belfast Loughs enabled her to grow sub-tropical acacias and lapagerias – the tender, rose-coloured climber also known as the Chilean bellflower, which would have struggled to survive at her chilly Scottish childhood home, Dunrobin Castle.

Elements of fantasy and symbolism can be found throughout these celebrated gardens. Extravagant planting embellishes the symmetry and stonework of the Italian Garden along the house's south front. The steps, balustrading and other stonework were inspired by Villa Gamberaia near Florence, while the design of the beds was adapted from Dunrobin; they are variously edged with low red berberis, dwarf rhododendrons and shrubby potentilla. Eastern and western parterres are divided by an emerald lawn, each with a central circular, stone lily pool. The parterres are not mirror images, but both are planted to represent the hues of sunrise and sunset on the lough. Structure comes in March and April from camellias and tender magnolias, followed by rhododendrons in May, then callistemons and the red and white flowers of clianthus, the lobster-claw shrub – another more tender specimen that thrives here. The dark-green, serrated leaves of evergreen loquat (*Eriobotrya japonica*) give year-round interest, with ripe orange fruits in spring and summer. Abutilons, cannas and the large-leafed Abyssinian banana are a dark summer foil for colourful summer planting.

An impressive *Cornus capitata*, covered in white flowers in June, stands by steps down to the Spanish Garden, where an oval pool is surrounded by hammered pebbles and urns of pelargoniums.

Extravagant planting embellishes the symmetry and stonework of the Italian Garden along the house's south front.

Bush wisterias, tree peonies and giant scarlet Mexican salvias are set against leylandii tightly clipped and resembling railway viaducts.

Leyland cypress (×*Cupressocyparis leylandii*) may be the bugbear of suburbia but it is used to great effect at Mount Stewart, while Chilean yew (*Prumnopitys andina*) encloses the west-facing Sunk Garden and its pergola on three sides. Four large geometric beds around another silky lawn are defined by low clipped bay and heather hedges, and planted primarily in blue and yellow (aconitum, delphiniums and phlox), matched by golden-yellow lilies above. Sub-tropical planting includes fluffy pink tamarisk and spiky

Above An aerial view of the Italian Garden shows the striking layout of the parterre beds, and the central grass avenue that is lined with *Cordyline australis*. Beyond is the Spanish Garden with its arcading of leylandii. To one side is a magnificently spreading hardy hybrid rhododendron.

Yucca gloriosa and *Y. filamentosa*, with white flower spires in summer. Clematis and fuchsia clamber along the pergola and on the terrace are umbrellas of bay.

The playful Shamrock Garden blends Scottish and Irish legends, among which you'll find the

Red Hand of Ulster laid out in bedding plants, along with a topiary harp for Ireland. A family hunting party is depicted in topiary, and on stone terraces above the Italian Garden are depictions of real and mythological animals, including crocodiles, dinosaurs and griffins.

The fine collection of rhododendrons appears throughout the gardens and woods. Benefiting, as did her gardening contemporaries, from the inrush of plants from across the world, Lady Londonderry grew many of the rhododendrons from seed collected by Frank Kingdon-Ward in the Far East between the 1920s and 1940s.

In 1956, she handed the garden to the National Trust 'to ensure that these gardens should be permanently preserved and maintained in the future'. Mike Buffin, head gardener since 2022, has focussed on refreshing them. 'Lady Londonderry's passion for collecting scented rhododendrons was surpassed only by her love of Asiatic and North American lilies and cardiocrinums,' he says. 'We have recreated the feel of her time by extensive planting of lilies for high summer.' In the Lily Wood, between the Italian and Shamrock Gardens, there are now 600 cardiocrinums and 1,000 different varieties of lilies, including *Lilium auratum*. With gold-speckled white flowers, it grows to a height of 8 feet.

The aim has always been to remain true to Lady Londonderry while responding to climate change and new plant material. As Mike notes: 'In this climate, you can grow an ever-increasing array of hardy and sub-tropical plants. If Lady Londonderry were alive today, I am sure she would embrace the opportunities a warming climate offers to a fun-loving plantaholic.'

Packwood House, Warwickshire

Packwood House has settled comfortably over the centuries into a sleepy Warwickshire hollow, with red brick walls softened by planting and always those magnificent topiary yews – perhaps one of Packwood's most intriguing features. This is not a grand mansion, but a squire's home divided from farm buildings and a walled kitchen garden by a country lane.

Between 1924 and 1931, Baron Ash, the son of a wealthy industrialist, took Packwood back to its Elizabethan roots by removing Georgian and Victorian additions and replacing later sash windows with leaded ones. His vision of improvement also took in the garden, noting its early 17th-century framework: the iconic Yew Garden, the front gazebo and the entrance court and kitchen garden walls all appear on a 1723 estate plan with many of the yews and much of the box hedging dating from the early 1600s. The result of Ash's work and most recently that of Mick Evans, head gardener from 2000–23, is a garden perfectly in sympathy with both house and parkland.

The curious collection of trees that make up the Yew Garden is known as the Sermon on the Mount – a 'multitude' of smaller yews lead up the slope towards the Master, reached by a box spiral and flanked by four Evangelist and 12 Apostle yews.

Yet this is more than a stand-alone feature; expectation builds towards it through clever use of colour, starting with pale blues and silver borders in the entrance court. The branches of a 19th-century 'Brown Turkey' fig on one wall are trained in elaborate spirals to draw attention to its leafless structure in winter.

A Sunken Garden, created by Baron Ash in the 1930s, has a stone-edged pool surrounded with raised beds of crushed brick. Planting has been adapted to drought-tolerant grasses, sempervivums, parahebes, deep blue *Eryngium* × *oliverianum* and fierce-looking Himalayan *Morina longifolia* with pink flowers.

Among the lawns of the Carolean Garden, borders are planted in the 'mingled' style, advocated by the early 19th-century garden writer and designer John Claudius Loudon in which individual plants or groups of plants are repeated through a border. A textured,

contemporary blend of hardy and tender perennials, annuals and wild flowers flourishes in the Yellow Border through supporting cages of hazel coppiced from the estate.

The Double Borders, along the stone path between the house and the Yew Garden, also reinterpret Loudon for the 21st century. Structural yucca, *Stipa gigantea* and cardoons are repeated – the golden hues of giant oat grass picking up on the render of the house, and the cardoons its silvery drainpiping and window frames. Among these uprights are lower-level perennials and annuals in pinks, purples and blues, and self-seeded echiums and poppies.

A semi-circle of red brick steps leads up to the hotter-coloured borders of the Raised Terrace planted in bronzes and reds. Evergreen laburnum, *Piptanthus nepalensis*, repeats on the diagonal along the borders. *Aeonium* 'Zwartkop' and *Phormium* 'Bronze Baby' pick out a copper

beech in the park, while fiery red *Hemerocallis* 'Stafford' and *Abutilon* 'Patrick Synge' tone with the garden walls. Tender perennials, such as cannas and tibouchina, are over-wintered in greenhouses before replacing tulips and wallflowers. 'In summer, we're planting out annuals,' says senior gardener Robyn Booth. 'Then in autumn we're cutting back, mulching, lifting and planting bulbs.'

Aeonium 'Zwartkop' and *Phormium* 'Bronze Baby' pick out a copper beech in the park, while fiery red *Hemerocallis* 'Stafford' and *Abutilon* 'Patrick Synge' tone with the garden walls.

Opposite Some yew shapes in Packwood's Sermon on the Mount garden possibly date from the early 1600s. A 10-year project began in 2014 to help regenerate yews struggling in heavy clay soil compacted by visitor numbers.

Right Pleached 'Golden Hornet' crab apples give year-round structure to the kitchen garden, as well as providing golden fruit in autumn. Planting mixes sunflowers, *Sidalcea* 'Party Girl', *Echinops* 'Veitch's Blue', self-seeded *Digitalis purpurea* and grape vines.

Below The Sunken Garden was originally laid out in the 1930s by Baron Ash with raised brick beds around a rectangular pool. Planting adapted to climate change features ant grasses, sisyrinchiums, self-seeded verbascums, *Stipa tenuissima* and *Erysimum* 'Bowles's Mauve'.

Across the lane from the house is the walled kitchen garden, a medley of flowers, fruit and vegetables. Robyn calls this her 'kingdom; a place to have fun and play with colour'. The garden was restored in 2012 and planted out with four main productive plots, as in the 1723 estate plan. A dipping pool of traditional lime mortar marks the centre while pleached 'Golden Hornet' crab apples and stepover and espaliered fruit add a framework. Robyn looks for diversity rather than quantity: she enjoys trialling new varieties, such as tomatillos or 'Nine Star' cauliflowers, short-lived perennials that produce several smaller heads over two or three years.

Globe artichokes, raspberries, strawberries, gooseberries, garlic, cherries and asparagus are mixed in one quarter; runner and broad beans, radishes, beetroot and herbs in another. Flowers add froth but also attract pollinators to tomatoes and pumpkins, and nasturtiums distract aphids and caterpillars. 'We are trying to keep things in balance,' explains Robyn. 'We don't use sprays, so accept a certain amount of damage.'

Running through wide central borders are 6-foot spears of purple-stemmed *Allium* 'Summer Drummer' and *Salvia sclarea* var. *turkestanica*, above self-seeded nigella, poppies, marigolds (to lure black fly away from beans) and *Achillea* 'Cerise Queen' for hoverflies and butterflies. As a guest in 1934 wrote in the visitors' book, Packwood is 'a house to dream of, a garden to dream in'. Centuries on, Packwood's history continues to grow and fulfil such garden dreams.

Above A *Catalpa bignonioides* 'Aurea' fronts a 17th-century gazebo. The Yellow Border is planted with nepeta, *Achillea* 'Cerise Queen', *Sidalcea* 'Party Girl', *Macleaya microcarpa* 'Kelway's Coral Plume', self-seeded oriental poppies and *Salvia sclarea* var. *turkestanica* 'Vatican Pink'.

Powis Castle, Powys

From its high crag, the 13th-century red sandstone fortress of Powis Castle towers over the Welsh Marches. Your first view is indeed unforgettable, as you spot the 30-foot yews bulging along the parapet-like, crenellated fortifications. Less immediately apparent are the extensive gardens. Combining Baroque style with sumptuous Edwardian planting, they tumble down through terraces towards orchards, rose borders and woodland. The high east terrace, punctuated by mop-head hollies in huge lead planters, commands views of the gardens below and over woodland and parkland towards Welshpool.

Combining Baroque style with sumptuous Edwardian planting, the gardens tumble down through terraces towards orchards, rose borders and woodland.

From the 1570s, the castle was owned by the Herbert family. In the late 17th and early 18th centuries, the Herberts built the Baroque terraces, with an aviary, orangery and Flemish lead statues along the balustrades. From there, yew hedges, thought to be contemporary with the parapet yews, run down the hill like breakwaters. When much of the garden languished during the Second World War, the yews were still clipped.

The terraces were turned into opulent flower gardens from 1911 by Violet, wife of the 4th Earl of Powis, but these had become neglected by the time the National Trust took over Powis in the 1970s. Head gardener David Swanton, who joined Powis in 1999, has maintained the Edwardian spirit of these vibrant borders, while introducing new, stronger cultivars. 'We tweak the borders and move something about each year,' he says. 'Our standards are very high.' The borders are time-consuming: filled with annuals and perennials, they need summer-long deadheading.

The hillside and yew hedging shelter the terraces from prevailing winds. Tender perennials flourish on the Upper Terrace against walls covered in white and mauve wisterias, some of them 200 years old. Other climbers include purple vines, clematis and roses. Winter-greenhoused cannas and bananas are introduced into the beds in May among hardier salvias and geraniums. Box edging is propagated at Powis to reduce the danger of importing box blight.

The right-hand Orangery Terrace and the Aviary Terrace opposite are daringly dissimilar. The former's Italianate atmosphere is enhanced by terracotta pots of citrus trees and beds full of hot-coloured perennial and annual planting. The Aviary Terrace, by contrast, is decked out in cool blues and whites, with climbing roses in toning colours behind. On the Lower Terrace,

Left The border by the gardener's bothy in the Lower Garden bulges with perennial salvias, achilleas, liatris, aconitum and tall, multi-coloured hollyhocks. Its informality contrasts with the planting in the Upper Garden.

Below Textured planting along the Orangery Terrace includes *Rosa* 'Buff Beauty', persicaria, salvias, atriplex, acanthus and poppies, with wisteria running along the walls behind.

below walls wrapped in 'Constance Spry' and 'Blairii Number Two' roses, are south-facing beds planted with hostas, euphorbia, *Salvia nemorosa* 'Caradonna', sedums and *Alchemilla mollis*.

As you descend the terraces, the ethos changes. The gardener's half-timbered bothy stands in the Lower Garden, where the planting is more country cottage in style. Square beds of golden marjoram, set in grass, are the footings for a vine tunnel near a recently introduced wildflower border. An orchard, originally planted by Lady Violet in the early 1900s, features heritage apple cultivars, such as 'Laxton's Superb', 'Bismarck', 'Lord Derby' and 'Rosemary Russet'. Old English roses, modern shrub and floribundas are planted in long borders among alliums for May, and pink, red and blue herbaceous planting (achilleas, delphiniums and campanulas) for summer.

David Swanton is proud of his work in the woodlands, where he took out stretches of *Rhododendron ponticum*, gave prominence to ancient oaks and two sequoias and released views towards both castle and countryside. 'It was very one-dimensional,' says David, 'but now there are more layers of interest.' Wild flowers are reappearing in cleared glades, with wood anemones and primroses flowering in spring, followed by ox-eye daisies.

There are orchids aplenty, too, including common spotted, marsh and (two-leafed) twayblade – satisfyingly tiny details set against the vast scale of Powis Castle.

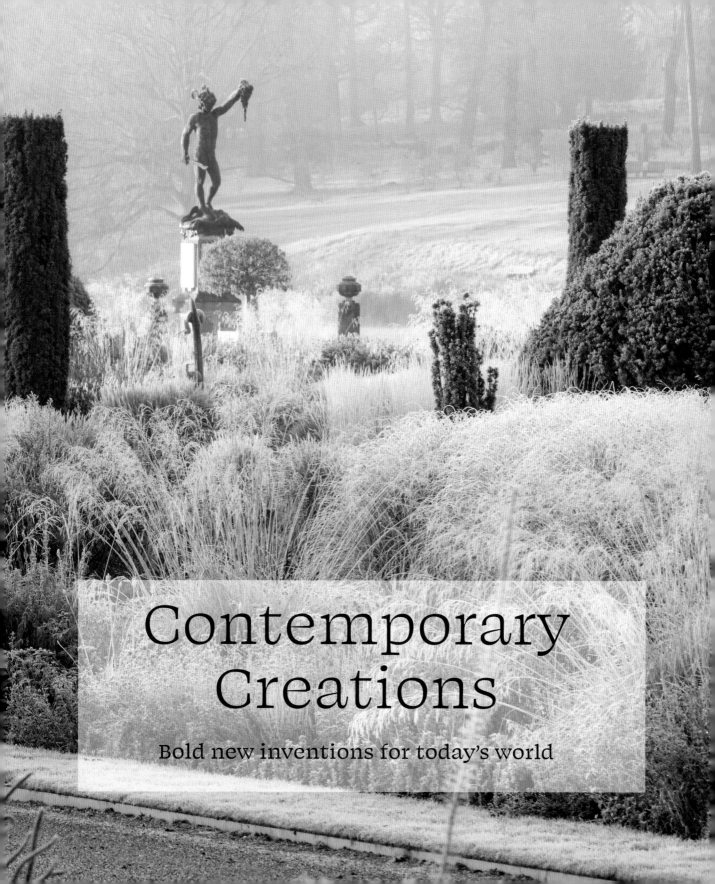

Contemporary Creations

Bold new inventions for today's world

Bourton House Garden, Gloucestershire

The gardening poet Alexander Pope believed that all good gardens should consult 'the genius of the place'. Bourton House Garden amply succeeds; land slants up to a wooded ridge and also falls away to fields of grazing cattle. Flower borders along an 18th-century walkway appear to drift out onto the Gloucestershire hillside.

Since 2010 Bourton House has been the home of Roelof and Cheryl Quintus, but the 3-acre garden was shaped by Monique Paice in the 1980s and 1990s. She covered the 18th-century house in tight lines of orange-berried pyracantha and made a sophisticated modern garden of lawns and flower borders to complement it. Working within existing Cotswold stone walls and remoulded yew hedging, she showcased the view across an immaculate lawn planted with two burnt-red *Parrotia persica*. As most of the trees – beech, yews, pillars of *Populus tremula* 'Erecta' and an exedra of *Malus floribunda* – are around the periphery, the garden has an open, sunny aspect.

The planting style was devised by Paul Williams, Mrs Paice's head gardener. His love

of tropical plants and container gardening still informs the garden, partly because of continuity: Jacky Rae, head gardener since 2018, worked for 15 years with her predecessor, Paul Nicholls, who had gardened with Williams.

The season begins gently with tulips, scillas and bluebells, but there is a late summer crescendo of overflowing borders and pots. This scintillating display is achieved by annually lifting then replanting tender cannas, bananas, agaves and aeoniums among shrubs, annuals and hardy perennials. This level of intervention is unusual in gardens today, but it ensures a kaleidoscope of colours, shapes and textures as new combinations are tried and plants relocated.

Bourton's distinctive quality is instantly apparent. By the entrance of the Grade I-listed tithe barn are pots piled with heliotrope, pelargoniums, fuchsias, diamond-leafed *Persicaria runcinata* 'Purple Fantasy' and fleshy *Impatiens sodenii*. Nearby in the Brewhouse garden, a dark bed is theatrically structured by hardy shrubs – fuchsia, bamboo, black elder and the giant reed

Arundo donax var. *versicolor* – among which are intermingled the strong colours of salvias, datura, *Dahlia* 'Arabian Night', *Abutilon* 'Nabob' and 'Red Tiger', heliotrope and the red and orange trumpets of *Cuphea micropetala*.

These themes continue through the Herbaceous Borders and in deep borders on three sides of the main lawn. In the Warm Border, shrubs including *Lonicera involucrata*, cornus, roses 'Buff Beauty' and yellow 'Arthur Bell' are the permanent backdrop to a changing cast of aeoniums and huge-leafed black and green bananas, grown from seed. Castor oil plants and amaranth, grown as annuals, and the yellow of heleniums, orange lantana and further hardy perennials complete the picture. Opposite, in the yew-backed West Border, roses, peonies, perovskia, sedums and salvias appear with tibouchina, brought out from the greenhouse in spring, along with phormiums, sumac and tetrapanax. To keep the planting schemes fresh, the three full-time gardeners annually take 2,000 cuttings.

Less intense in its colouring is the Topiary Garden, where spirals and roundels of box, and pots of white marguerites within box buttresses lead towards *Hydrangea arborescens* 'Annabelle' grouped along a wall. Through ogee-shaped yews, you glimpse the White Garden's double borders, set off by 'Iceberg' and horizontal 'Max Graf' roses, *Argyranthemum frutescens* 'Quinta White', crinums and phlox.

Most change has been gradual, but two areas have had to be transformed more urgently. Blight destroyed the box in the Knot Garden

In the Topiary Garden, spirals and roundels of box, and pots of white marguerites within box buttresses lead towards *Hydrangea arborescens* 'Annabelle' grouped along a wall.

Opposite In the Parterre Garden, where the box parterre was lost to blight, wild flowers now add informality to the remaining yew and prunus topiary.

Left Tender perennials, such as the Ethiopian black banana (*Ensete ventricosum*), aeoniums and *Agave attenuata*, are over-wintered and then planted out in the Warm Border for summer with *Dahlia* 'David Howard', green ensete and *Crocosmia* 'Lucifer'.

Below In the White Garden, annuals, perennials and *Dahlia* 'Waterlily White' are planted among *Anemone* 'Honorine Jobert' and the double *A.* 'Whirlwind'. Mopheads of *Syringa* 'Madame Lemoine' stand at the corners of the spring-fed pool.

and Parterre over the winter of 2021–22, necessitating a complete rethink. 'It was heart-breaking, but it was a new opportunity,' says Jacky. 'It's how gardens progress.'

In the Knot Garden, panels of different-coloured grasses have replaced the box. An inner circle of *Calamagrostis brachytricha* matches the bulrush plumes of *Scirpus lacustris* in the basketwork pond made for the 1851 Great Exhibition. The Parterre is even more of a

departure: where there were once spirals and cones of box is now a meadow of umbellifers, poppies, cornflowers and other wild flowers. Two central lines of summer-flowering *Daphne* 'Eternal Fragrance' and encircling rows of dwarf yew *Taxus baccata* 'Renke's Kleiner Grüner' strike the only formal note. The effect is charming, but very different from its predecessor.

If you have time, wander along the bumpy paths through the long grass in the adjacent 7-acre field, planted up in 1994–95. There are now maturing groups of birch, ornamental pears, flowering crab apples, walnuts, hawthorn, larches, toffee-scented katsura (*Cercidiphyllum japonicum*), hazels and willows. The field is a sea of white blossom in May, then later in the year a green counterpart to its brighter neighbour.

Above Variously sized and vivid containers by the entrance to the garden are an earnest of things to come. Purple heliotrope is mixed with orange lantana, cerise fuchsia and other tender planting in a glorious curtain-raising display.

East Ruston Old Vicarage, Norfolk

Surely Alan Gray and Graham Robeson were theatrical impresarios in some earlier life. Over the 32 acres of this generous, near-coastal garden, they direct visitors from one set-piece to another, using walls and beech hedging like elements of stage scenery. The drama builds from the changes of aspect – between, for instance, brick-stepped terraces in the Mediterranean Garden and the adjacent Desert Wash, resembling Arizona with its agaves, yuccas, cacti and palms.

The year 2023 marked half a century since the couple bought East Ruston Old Vicarage, an Arts and Crafts house with 2 acres standing shelterless in a lowland, 25 miles north-east of Norwich. Since then, they have bought more

Above The Dutch Garden is a formal area of clipped and layered holly, roundels of box and yew cones. Tender planting includes orange marigolds, *Ensete ventricosum* 'Maurelii' and various dahlias.

Left Within the south-facing walled areas of the Mediterranean Garden are planted *Echium pininana*, euphorbia, *Lobelia tupa*, spiky Mexican *Beschorneria yuccoides*, salvias, escallonia and vigorously self-seeding fennel.

Below East Ruston Old Vicarage is a garden of vistas framed by brick archways and by hedging. Set in a lily pond in the Sunk Garden is an abstract stainless steel and glass sculpture by Bill Cordaroy.

land on which they continually test out what plants will do. 'Once we started pushing out the boundaries of tenderness,' Alan explains, 'we kept pushing. Also the climate has changed radically in 50 years and has become more amenable to half-hardies. We wouldn't have put a pittosporum outside in 1973.'

East Ruston benefits from free-draining, light loam soil and being only a mile from the North Sea. 'There is a slip of coast from just north of here down to Lowestoft that gets the same number of frost days as Devon and Cornwall,' says Graham. Bamboo, gunnera, ligularia, phormiums and tree ferns (which aren't covered in winter) have long been happy growing here. A newer, more typically half-hardy introduction is *Erythrina crista-galli*, a South American native, with bunches of red flowers like lobster claws. When he stops to talk, Alan is tying in its long, fragile shoots to prevent them breaking off in the wind that is always an enemy in Norfolk – despite shelter belts of Monterey pines (*Pinus radiata*), Italian alders (*Alnus cordata*), holm oaks and eucalyptus.

There are tranquil passages of beech, holm oaks and acacia, and, in a garden mostly looking inwards, sudden prospects of East Ruston and Happisburgh churches and of Happisburgh Lighthouse through lunettes in the hedging or

'There is a slip of coast from just north of here down to Lowestoft that gets the same number of frost days as Devon and Cornwall.'

along avenues. From enclosed rooms around the house, the garden opens out towards a woodland, spring walk, wilderness, wildflower meadow, serpentine birch walk and wildlife pond. Pollarded Italian alders enclose rectangles of meadow grass with crocus, narcissus and camassias. Cowslips and knapweed then appear

in the rectangles that are mown in August ready for autumn crocus.

The couple's constant urge to reinvent has led to later walled additions towards the garden's periphery. These include the walled Fruit Cage and Dahlia Border and a garden created in 2012 for the late Queen's Diamond Jubilee with a glasshouse, central rose arch and climber-clad walls.

The enclosed Dutch Garden was designed outside their drawing room in the 1980s with red brick paths, pots of brugmansia and their dramatic trumpet flowers in summer, box topiary and flowering annuals following on

from spring tulips. The garden's central axis, the King's Walk, is planted with ten triangular yews backed by beech hedging and its plain expanse of lawn punctuated by sets of low steps. Beyond a wisteria-covered pavilion is the Mediterranean Garden, where hedging was replaced by a wall in 2024 and what Alan describes as 'a monumental entrance' erected. 'You now unexpectedly enter the Desert Wash through a green court. We've planted agaves against the south-facing wall and increased the bulbs here with autumn zephyranthes ('flowers of the west wind').'

In the Catalpa Garden, 16 standard, August-flowering *Catalpa bignonioides* (Indian Bean trees) stand in a grid, the attention shared in spring with hellebores and narcissi beneath. Alan and Graham have kept digging: the Sunk Garden is as much as 5 feet below ground level, so feels several degrees warmer in winter. Roses are planted with *Lobelia tupa*, *Azara microphylla* and grasses. *Escallonia bifida*, a somewhat tender shrub, grows in a sheltered corner by a south wall. Domed with white blossom in October, it is a magnet for late butterflies.

In the Exotic Garden, approached via a sizeable Japanese-style pergola, outsized leaves create a jungly feel: *Tetrapanax papyrifer* 'Rex' and bananas (hardy *Musa basjoo* and tender red-leafed *Ensete maurelii* that needs lifting in winter). A waterspout fountain stands in one of two raised ponds, the other dedicated to wildlife and with a surface of water lilies.

Most impressive is the sheer quality of horticulture. Alan claims that 'my favourite bit is always what I'm working on. I'm constantly trying to improve and to refine the plant varieties.' It has been important to both Alan and Graham 'to make a safe haven in an ever more hostile world'. That refuge is now secure, as East Ruston has been bequeathed on their deaths to the gardening charity, Perennial, which will, in due course, look after this unique garden for future generations.

Opposite Behind Piet Oudolf's Floral Labyrinth is the clock tower – a vestige of the razed mansion. Semi-transparent grasses, *Sesleria autumnalis*, *Molinia* subsp. *arundinacea* 'Transparent' and stipa, weave through panicum, miscanthus and perennials (*Koenigia divaricata*, persicaria, *Filipendula rubra* 'Venusta' and *Solidago* x *luteus* 'Lemore').

Trentham, Staffordshire

Titans meet at Trentham – and provide a mighty spectacle for garden lovers. Lake and parkland were modelled by 'Capability' Brown between 1759 and 1780 and the mansion and terracing were designed in the favoured Italianate style of the 1830s for the 2nd Duke of Sutherland by Sir Charles Barry, architect of the Houses of Parliament. Forward to the 21st century and in 2003 to 2004 the gardens were redesigned with contemporary European-steppe planting by Piet Oudolf and Tom Stuart-Smith, international garden designers and Chelsea Flower Show gold medal winners. And in 2016, a perennial meadow between the lake and river was added by Nigel Dunnett, Professor of Planting Design at the University of Sheffield and a designer of the 2012 London Olympics parkland.

Entrance to the gardens at Trentham is across a wooden bridge over the River Trent. Dragonflies dance beneath willows along the crystal-clear water, but it was not ever thus. The Potteries that made Staffordshire's fortune also polluted its rivers. George Fleming, the 2nd Duke's head gardener, diverted the Trent to stop it silting up, but could do nothing about the stench. The mansion was razed in 1911, leaving just the Hall's grand *porte-cochère* entrance, the semi-circular sweep of the Orangery, and a side wing with Ionic pilasters and a clock tower.

Trentham's reconstruction was a £100m project by St Modwen Properties who bought the dilapidated estate in 1996 to develop it as a tourist destination. While the mansion remains undeveloped, the ruins give focus to the Italian Garden, resurrected between mansion and lake and now planted with 80,000 perennials in over 400 different varieties in 70 flowerbeds. There is no understatement at Trentham.

The sense of drama begins with Oudolf's Rivers of Grasses. These whirling perennials and grasses are a particular favourite of Trentham gardener, Jolene Lowndes, who loves 'the different heights and textures'. Roundels of dark green *Amsonia tabernaemontana* var. *salicifolia* give shape to sweeps of persicaria, astilbes, salvias,

Left In a corner of Oudolf's Floral Labyrinth by a containing beech hedge, umbellifers, salvias, *Aster* x *frikartii* 'Mönch', purple monardas, phlomis seedheads and persicaria come together in a joyous harmony.

Below Oudolf's colourful borders of eupatorium, alliums and blue *Phlox paniculata* 'Lichtspel' frame Stuart-Smith's central, grass-dominated planting on the lower terrace of the Italian Garden.

Opposite The stark simplicity of Stuart-Smith's overall design for the Italian Garden is apparent in mid-winter when yew shapes and fountains of grass dominate both the Lower and Upper Terraces.

umbellifers and grasses such as *Molinia caerulea*. Verdant in spring, these beds turn a rich russet as the summer progresses and impact comes as much from seedheads as from flower colour.

A semi-circular grove of rough-stemmed water birches (*Betula occidentalis*) divides the Rivers of Grasses from the Floral Labyrinth where paths weave between 32 ingeniously planted beds. You brush through weeping miscanthus and view fluffy Finnish knotweed (*Koenigia divaricata*) amid head-high planting of eupatoriums, veronicastrums and sanguisorbas. Below are knautias, *Allium sphaerocephalon*, heleniums, achilleas and an edging of origanum, alive with bees.

The big reveal comes when you stand on the terrace fronting the mansion's ruins and look down on the balustraded Italian Garden. A broad central avenue, marked by Versailles planters of Portuguese laurels, leads to a mighty bronze statue of Perseus and Medusa on the lakeside. This Grade II-listed replica

The big reveal comes when you stand on the terrace fronting the mansion's ruins and look down on the balustraded Italian Garden.

of Benvenuto Cellini's 1550 masterwork was commissioned by the 2nd Duke of Sutherland and has been restored as the focal point of the majestic parterre.

It was a brilliant conception to reinterpret Barry's terraces on a similarly commanding scale – but where once there was carpet-bedding, to plant instead perennials and grasses. Oudolf's bolder strokes in the side beds complement Stuart-Smith's more precise central planting. Around the fountain on the Upper Terrace are roundels of yew and huge sprays of *Stipa*

Above In August, hard outlines are blurred, grasses are beginning to brown, and colour comes from a riotous display of *Crocosmia* 'Lucifer' and yellow rudbeckias and achilleas.

gigantea in wedges of mown grass. The shape of fountain and grasses is picked up by copper rose supports in surrounding beds, among blue, silver and white planting and low box domes.

On the Lower Terrace, planting is laid around 40 pillars of fastigiate Irish yew that echo Barry's original Italian cypresses. Structural amsonias and eupatorium reflect domed golden yews, while alchemilla, fennel, euphorbia and giant scabious match their colour.

The abstract lines of Stuart-Smith's design are clearly visible in winter and in spring when the tulips flower, but these are concealed as salvias, geraniums, monardas, inulas, helianthus, crocosmia, heleniums and grasses, all chosen for the dry conditions, fill out. The beds, set in Corten steel-edged lawns, are larger than in Barry's day, so visitors are now closer to the plants. As Stuart-Smith says: 'The experience of nature is very, very different. You're always hugely aware of the growth and height in the garden as well as the seasonal change.'

The magisterial contemporary design of Oudolf's Floral Labyrinth and Stuart-Smith's elegant terraces give way to the refilled, mile-long lake of 'Capability' Brown, now edged with Dunnett's sweeping meadows. The 752-acre estate also includes the hilly King's Wood, a night-green curtain above the lake and a Site of Special Scientific Interest.

While the shopping village, garden centre (both bordering the garden's entrance), lakeside walks and restaurants are invariably busy, Trentham is always magical. Even in high summer, you can find yourself almost alone – hidden within grassy spaces amid sinuous planting.

Wildside, Devon

Above In the Courtyard, golden variegated aralias frame the glaucous-leafed *Kniphofia caulescens* 'John May' with bronze *Carex comans* in the foreground. Large-leafed small trees evoke the Mediterranean and southern hemisphere.

Wildside is an outstanding, modern naturalistic garden created by Keith and Ros Wiley since 2004. Three distinct areas have been ingeniously sculpted to give the conditions that an impressive array of plants would enjoy in the wild.

Starting in the Lower Garden, a grove of 60 Japanese maples shade woodland plants collected by Keith while head gardener at The Garden House nearby from 1978 to 2003. Interlocking banks mirror the domes of the

maples that stream through the garden in a ribbon of red, green and yellow. A wedding-cake cornus (*Cornus controversa* 'Variegata'), planted at 3 foot, is now a 30 foot tree. 'I love seeing its structure through the silver leaves,' says Keith. For him, shape is all-important, and as trees mature, he gradually removes lower branches to reveal their trunks. Groups of conifers and cornus grown close together arch out and form a single unit. Several compactly planted *Magnolia*

stellata form a framework for early snowdrops and erythroniums, with a contrasting pink-flowered *Styrax japonicus* 'Benibana'. There are 80 magnolias in the Lower Garden – pink, white and yellow in spring; as they grow they will raise the canopy of the garden.

Paths wind up and down between the banks, passing a small orchard of cider apple trees, sole survivors from before the Wileys' intervention. The ripe fruit is not picked but left on the trees for redwings and fieldfares. A cut-leaf crab apple, *Malus transitoria*, with bonfire-red leaves in autumn, sprawls near one path, moss on its gnarled branches conferring a patina of age.

The ground drops away to a stone wall at head height, out of which poke oak tree roots (of which more later), and where a water garden, framed by broad-leafed magnolias, calls to mind a Devon valley. Snowdrops and wood anemones run down to the water, covered later by the foliage of rodgersias and hedychiums.

As you zig-zag past stands of scented azaleas, the tiered planting evokes a natural woodland. Enter the Courtyard, the middle of the three areas, and there is a volte face. Keith describes this cloister-like area surrounded by pergolas of wisteria as 'a smoothie version of all the places we've been on holiday'. The ochre-rendered walls were inspired by the colours of Bryce Canyon in Utah, while stone and terracotta olive jars amid the planting, again in interlocking shapes, recall the Mediterranean. Tall *Cordyline australis* stand

Above The Wileys built their home overlooking the Canyon Gardens where naturalistic planting features hemerocallis and many different grasses, including miscanthus varieties and *Stipa gigantea*. Yellow *Euphorbia sikkimensis*, *Hemerocallis citrina* and *Crocosmia* 'Lucifer' punctuate the greenery.

Opposite Stony paths plunge through a rich tapestry of grasses and perennials, including crocosmias, coreopsis and the early sprays of *Campanula lactiflora*. Birches thrive in the poor soil and provide an attractive canopy for the planting.

in the four stone-edged, raised beds, reframing views of self-seeded agapanthus, lilies, grasses, small-flowered gladioli, silvery perovskias and late summer roscoeas. Another viewing angle is between the rough-textured trunks of three *Cupressus cashmeriana*.

The dynamic alters again in the Canyons. This third area is a landscape with fewer trees and swirling banks of agapanthus, crocosmias, dieramas, dahlias and grasses such as molinia and miscanthus planted for movement. Along one bank grow just six cistus, happy on an airy site with poor soil and no shade: in May, you can't put a pin through their blanket of white flowers.

The Ros Wiley Tribute Garden is a dramatic canyon at the heart of this area, created in memory of Keith's artist wife who died in September 2019. Conjuring up South Africa, it rises in a series of four decreasing-sized ovals, with more meshing banks of conifers and self-seeded birches. Water is propelled over cascades, stepped rocks and through channels down to a pool by two pumps to give both a trickling and deep-throated sound. The valley is studded with the bright colours Ros loved and used in her paintings – kniphofias, gladioli, dark blue shrubby salvias, osteospermums and scarlet gazanias. Stony soil concentrates your eye on tiny spikes of amaryllis, zephyrlily and *Roscoea purpurea* 'Ros Wiley'.

Reaching an observation point, with a 360° panorama over Dartmoor and towards Plymouth and the coast 7 miles away, you are met with a 25-foot drop to the lane. This is where the Wileys' full achievement hits you. The 3-acre field was completely flat when the Wileys bought it: all the banks, valleys and dells you have wandered through were dug out and formed by Keith and Ros. 'We stripped soil off the entire field, then shaped the landscape (the fun part) before reintroducing the soil,' explains Keith. 'In

'I am trying to unlock the limitless possibilities of gardening and set people's imaginations free.'

places, it was laid to a few inches, in others 6 foot. We shifted about 150,000 tons of soil and shillet (degraded slate).'

The stone walls mentioned earlier are of this degraded slate, their top surface covered with 7 inches of soil at head height – you now stand well below the level of the field 20 years ago. Keith's excavations exposed the oak tree roots (and those of the birches in the Tribute Garden) and those roots hold the banks together. Keith has reshaped his landscape as comprehensively as

'Capability' Brown did in the 18th century. He has even adopted Brownian techniques: small trees planted on mounds or hillocks and half-hidden by others appear from a distance taller and more mature.

Underneath the shillet in the Tribute Garden are 90 tons of coarse sand, the texture of demerara sugar, for improved drainage. The addition of leaf mould and soil to the shillet has allowed damp-loving rodgersias to put their roots down to find moisture, and woodland plants such as erythroniums to grow in stones and among grasses. 'Creating many different conditions proves plants' adaptability,' concludes Keith. 'I am trying to unlock the limitless possibilities of gardening and set people's imaginations free.'

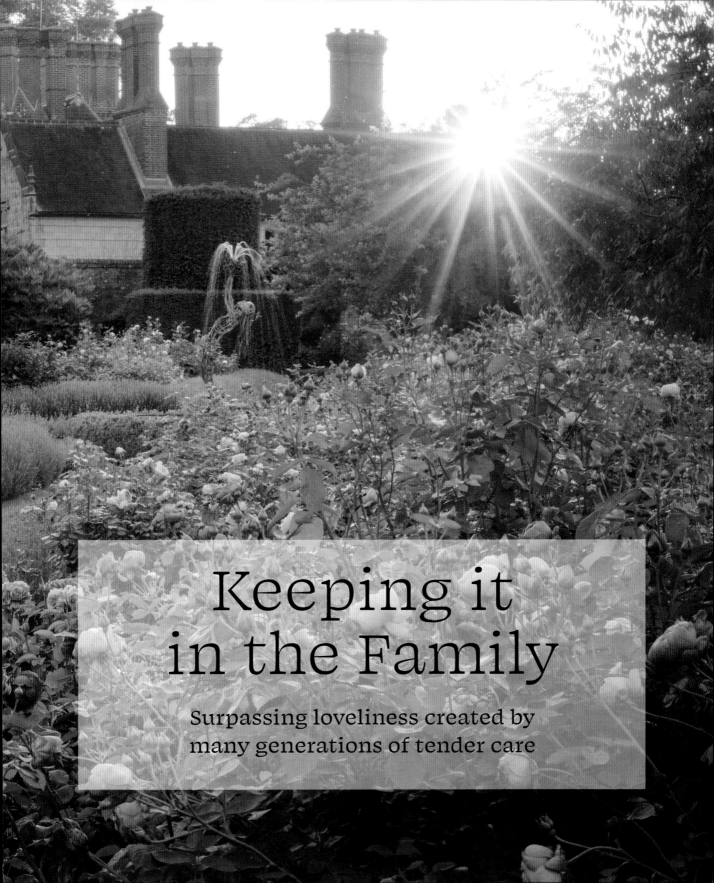

Keeping it in the Family

Surpassing loveliness created by
many generations of tender care

Borde Hill, West Sussex

In March, the goddess magnolia (*Magnolia sprengeri* var. *diva*) soars above the entrance to Borde Hill, its leafless branches covered with rich pink blooms. Beyond are more magnolias, from pure white to full pink, some with dark red centres, others with tissue paper flowers. These statuesque trees are among the spring highlights at Borde Hill, but two months later the picture has changed: in the Old Rhododendron Garden the magnolias, now in full leaf, have become a canopy for crimson *Rhododendron barbatum* and mauvy-white *R. fortunei*, both introduced from China in the 19th century.

They were planted in the 1900s by Colonel Stephenson Robert Clarke, who bought the Elizabethan mansion in the Sussex High Weald in 1893, knowing that the range of soils and conditions across the 380-acre estate would suit many types of plants. Over the next 50 years, he supported plant hunters in the Far East and South America and corresponded and swapped plants with other collectors and with the botanic gardens at Kew and Edinburgh. In the process, he assembled one of the UK's finest collections of rare trees and flowering shrubs still in private hands.

The house looks to the north towards the Ouse Valley Viaduct, a graceful 1840s structure that rises out of early mist on a summer's morning. To the south, Colonel Clarke unfolded views over parkland past a centuries-old oak by flattening the ground and laying an apron of lawn. Along two sides, he planted rhododendrons, camellias and a rare catalpa (*Catalpa bungei* Duclouxii Group) with veined pink flowers, collected in western China in about 1900. He also created the Azalea Ring, a feast of orange, red and yellow in May and home to *Magnolia campbellii*, one of Borde Hill's more than 70 champion trees (registered as the largest in the UK by girth or height), with large pink flowers in spring. Planted here in 1928 and also hailing from China, *Emmenopterys henryi* took 83 years before it flowered in 2011, but has since put forth its creamy blooms during August several times.

In the sandy soil of the Garden of Allah, Colonel Clarke planted many magnolias, including a notable trio known affectionately

as the 'Three Sisters', all champions by girth. This late-flowering group comprises *Magnolia officinalis*, collected in China by Ernest Wilson, *M. fraseri* from the south-eastern USA, and *M. obovata* from Japan. The Chinese tulip tree (*Liriodendron chinense*), now more than 60 feet high, flowered here for the first time in cultivation in 1927. A spring star is the warm pink *Camellia × williamsii* 'Donation', a worldwide bestseller raised by Colonel Clarke's gardener, Walter Fleming, over the winter of 1937–38.

Colonel Clarke turned two former quarries into gardens: the Long Dell, where he planted rhododendrons; and the Round Dell, a damp, secluded spot suitable for sub-tropical

Above Red brick paths lined with *Lavandula angustifolia* 'Loddon Blue' run through Jay Robin's Rose Garden and converge on a fountain statue of Aphrodite by Brendon Murless.

planting. Woodlands beyond the 17-acre formal garden became home to more magnolias and rhododendrons, and to pines, pieris and the May-flowering handkerchief tree, *Davidia involucrata*.

Three successive generations have played their part. The colonel's son, Sir Ralph Stephenson Clarke, set up a charitable trust in 1965 to keep Borde Hill in the family at a point in its history when other Sussex gardens, including Nymans (see pp. 24–28), were being given to the National Trust. Ralph's son, Robert, a collector

Right The North Park can be glimpsed through the branches of the 'Three Sisters' late-flowering magnolias; champions by girth and between them representing China, the USA and Japan.

Below The Round Dell, a home for sub-tropical planting since the early 1900s, was redesigned in 2017. Now, a concrete arrow plunges towards a waterfall fountain through lush pittosporum, *Fatsia japonica*, ferns and rodgersias.

A rill runs down into a pool surrounded by pines, eucalyptus, cherries and magnolias, and by parterres of clipped box and yew.

and hybridiser like his grandfather, introduced American rhododendron species and set about cataloguing the collection. After Robert's premature death in 1987, his son, Andrewjohn, put the garden on a sound commercial footing by opening it to the public for much of the year.

Andrewjohn and his wife, Eleni, have introduced designed flower gardens set within Colonel Clarke's collections. A favourite with visitors is Jay Robin's Rose Garden, designed in 1996, and named after Andrewjohn and Eleni's then-teenaged daughter. Planted with 750 repeat-flowering David Austin roses bordered by lavender, the garden brims with scent and colour from June to September.

Different areas segue into one another. Take the Paradise Walk, a wall-backed bed of strong blue and yellow perennials, designed on the diagonal by Chris Beardshaw in 2020. It links acers on the woody West Bank with the formal Italian Garden, where a rill runs down into a pool surrounded by pines, eucalyptus, cherries and magnolias, and by parterres of clipped box and yew. Further down the Paradise Walk, you move from the Mediterranean to the sub-tropics and the Round Dell, taking an arrow-shaped concrete path, designed in 2017, that plunges into opulent green planting.

The effect of Andrewjohn and Eleni's work has been to extend the season of what was once mainly a spring garden into somewhere with appeal from February to October. Their continued involvement is what makes Borde Hill special, as Andrewjohn says: 'From childhood, I was always conscious of Borde Hill being very much a family home.'

Caerhays Castle, Cornwall

Caerhays is only a few miles from Truro, Cornwall's county town, yet somehow these woodland gardens feel more remote. Rugged rather than manicured, they form a dramatic backdrop to the grey stone medieval-style castle set in an elbow of hills above Porthluney beach. The castle was designed by John Nash in the early 1800s, its expense so great that it helped impoverish the Trevanions, who had lived here for centuries. They sold Caerhays to the Williams family and John Charles Williams, known as 'JC' (1861–1939), began creating gardens from coastal scrub in the 1880s.

The gardens enjoy a damp, frost-free climate, protection from south-westerly winds and an acidic, free-draining soil ideal for woodland planting. The valley is a bowl of colour when Caerhays is open from mid-February to mid-June. Early camellias are followed by magnolias, daffodils, then primroses. By late March, you can spot the pale yellow, droplet-like blooms of *Stachyurus*, catch the vanilla fragrance of tiny *Azara microphylla* flowers and admire the dark-purple blooms of *Magnolia* 'Caerhays Surprise', a 1959 cross, which is also ideal for smaller gardens. Scented rhododendrons, such as the white *Rhododendron* 'Fragrantissimum' and pinker *R.* 'Lady Alice Fitzwilliam', start flowering in April, while in May, banks are covered with bluebells and wild garlic. A choice of routes leads through the woods, with the sea often in sight between broadleaved trees and pines.

Above Tucked into its romantic woodland, Caerhays looks like a castle from medieval legend. In fact, it was designed in the early 1800s by John Nash.

four expeditions before Forrest's death in China in 1932. The collection's core is still formed by acers, cherries, styrax, sorbus, catalpa, camellias, magnolias and rhododendrons grown here from seed gathered by Wilson and Forrest.

This Grade II-listed garden is maintained today with the same passionate commitment by JC's great-grandson, Charles H. Williams, who holds the Royal Horticultural Society's Victoria Medal of Honour and owns Burncoose Nurseries near Redruth. Knowledge has been passed down between just four head gardeners over some 120 years: Jaimie Parsons, head gardener since 1994, learned from his predecessor, Philip Tregunna.

As a boy in the 1960s, Charles spent hours with Tregunna, an accomplished hybridiser. Later, as his father was involved in public life, Charles had a free hand in running the estate, so he has 'plotted and planned the planting here for 40 years'. His tenure has seen 'a great deal of rethinking. The Wilson/Forrest rhododendrons were in their prime in the 1960s and 70s,' explains Charles, 'but probably only 10 per cent of them were still growing here by 2018. We had to get propagating much faster.'

Scented rhododendrons start flowering in April, while in May, banks are covered with bluebells and wild garlic.

JC's initial interest was in hybridising daffodils, and some of his varieties survive among the 10,000 naturalised through the grounds. But his attention was soon captured by the work of Ernest Wilson and George Forrest, whose hazardous plant-hunting expeditions to remote areas of China introduced tree and shrub species that were suited to the conditions at Caerhays. JC was sole sponsor of Forrest's 1912–15 expedition and contributed to his subsequent

Left The gateway to the castle is bordered by a splendid *Rhododendron* 'Cornish Red' and great banks of daffodils.

Below The woodland is carpeted in spring with a rich covering of rhododendron petals, such as those that have fallen from *Rhododendron* 'Mrs Butler' (available from Burncoose Nurseries).

Opposite Caerhays Castle, framed by a blue Atlas cedar (*Cedrus atlantica* 'Glauca'), faces south-west over the sea; both the castle and its woodlands protected from north-east winds by the enfolding hillside behind.

The hurricane of January 1990 cleared about 20 per cent of the garden and presented new areas for planting. Jaimie and his team now care for 140 rather than 60 acres, having taken in the Old Park, which had become neglected since the 1960s. This expansion has enabled the creation of new collections, including *Enkianthus*, *Podocarpus* and some 20 species of *Carpinus*. Existing collections remain key too: Caerhays' National Collection of Magnolias numbers some 90 species and hundreds more cultivars and unnamed seedlings. Many came direct from China via Wilson and Forrest, including *Magnolia delavayi* in the woodland and on the front wall of the castle. Other historic introductions include rich pink magnolias, such as *M. dawsoniana*, fragrant white *M. doltsopa* and the pinky-white chalice flowers of *M.* × *veitchii*, planted in 1921. More recent are *M.* 'Julian Williams', with pink handkerchief-like flowers and named for Charles' father, while a *M. sargentiana* var. *robusta* was planted by Queen Elizabeth the Queen Mother in 1981.

Charles works with botanic gardens in the Far East, both for Caerhays and Burncoose Nurseries. 'Plant hunters are now getting into North Vietnam, on the same latitude that Wilson and Forrest were working, and they're finding new species of magnolia.'

With the future in mind, 65 varieties of *Malus* were planted in the former kitchen garden in early 2023 as part of the Queen's Green Canopy, a nationwide tree-planting initiative. In another 10-acre area, Kennel Close, young acers are being nurtured behind a protective windbreak of holm oak and an understorey of bay laurels. Nursery beds, tucked in among other planting, are filled with little rhododendrons, kept there for two to five years until they are planted in their final position.

Caerhays is an ever-evolving garden that offers endless variety between the historic woodland of camellias, magnolias and rhododendrons and the cleared glades of exciting new planting.

Opposite Magnificent white wrought-iron gates and screen, surmounted by the Cholmondeley's coat of arms, were made by Robert Bakewell in 1722 to mark the north entrance to the old hall. Since moved, gates and screen form a beautiful backdrop to spring daffodils.

Cholmondeley Castle Gardens, Cheshire

The formal gardens at Cholmondeley Castle in Cheshire are away from the hilltop castle and seem almost suspended in a dell within wildflower meadows. Standing near intricate, white, wrought-iron gates, adrift in a sea of daffodils in spring, you see the castle half-hidden by trees up to your right. Below are the lake, rose gardens and herbaceous borders, tantalisingly glimpsed beyond yew hedging.

> Standing near intricate, white, wrought-iron gates, adrift in a sea of daffodils in spring, you see the castle half-hidden by trees up to your right.

Much of this is the work of Lavinia, wife of Hugh, 6th Marquess of Cholmondeley, whose family have lived here since Norman times. Gardening runs in the blood: Lavinia's son, the present marquess, shares a passion for spring-flowering shrubs with Barry Grain, head gardener since 2013: through the 70 acres of gardens are now some 70 cornus, 70 cherries, 140 magnolias and 250 rhododendrons and azaleas, many of which are additions to those originally planted by Lady Lavinia.

While the family continuity is long, the castle itself dates only from the early 19th century, built using stones from a 17th-century house on the estate, with turrets later added to give it its fortified appearance. Lavinia arrived here in 1949 claiming not to know a pansy from a peony, but determined to 'create a garden of great romance'. The Glade she laid out is an archipelago of island beds on sheltered slopes that suit magnolias and camellias. Smaller plants are often half-obscured by taller ones. 'Lady Lavinia didn't like set levels,' explains Barry, 'preferring a mix of heights and for plants to grow as they do in the wild.' The Japanese, damp-shade lover, *Kirengeshoma palmata*, has yellow flowers in July and August, and good foliage on black stems for longer interest. *Clerodendrum trichotomum*, from the lower Himalayan slopes, has fragrant, white star

are darker in the centre, moving out to paler colours. Bearded irises, salvias, peonies and alliums introduce blue around the roses, and non-repeating roses and box cubes are planted in the hedge-backed beds amid *Alchemilla mollis*, phlox and hellebores, with taller eremurus and delphiniums.

The commemorative Lavinia Walk was extended from short existing borders in 2018. Its entrance is grandly flanked by early 18th-century statues of putti supporting baskets of flowers and fruit. Once in the borders, formality and informality run into one another, for just beyond are wildflower meadows, not mown until August. 'Fifty per cent of what is now meadow was once close-cut grass, but we didn't have the staff to cut it during the Covid-19 lockdowns,' says Barry. This has given the gardens their romantic, floating appearance and has also increased biodiversity: orchids are appearing everywhere and hares are breeding again on the estate.

Box hedging is laid out at calf-height in a Greek key design, but the hot-coloured planting is not shut away and is visible from the drive and main rooms of the castle. Sixteen *Malus hupehensis* crab apples give spring and autumn colour, while rose-covered obelisks, made by a local blacksmith, run through the beds. Planting is designed for long appeal, starting with tree peonies and bearded irises, then rising to a high-summer pinnacle of velvety dahlias, bright salvias,

flowers, whose dark pink calyx and then metallic blue berries carry on colour into autumn.

The Rose Garden was designed in 1952, but only a few of the older varieties and the warm pink colour scheme were retained when the garden was replanted over the winter of 2016–17. David Austin roses were introduced to extend the flowering season and ramble over wooden pergolas and arches. Adjacent, on a former tennis court, is a new rose garden, surrounded by yew that will eventually match the height of the hedge around its neighbouring garden. A *tempietto* (small temple) and Four Seasons statues, originally from Houghton Hall in Norfolk (the family's second seat), create an Italianate feel. Eight beds of repeating roses

Above In spring, the banks of the lake are lined with colourful *Prunus* x *yedoensis*, purple heathers and various Kurume azaleas. The statue is of an unnamed gladiator; the *tempietto* has now been moved to the new Rose Garden.

Right The Rose Garden was designed by Lady Cholmondeley in 1952 and replanted with repeat-flowering David Austin roses in 2016–17. The left-hand arch is covered with *Rosa* Super Fairy and the right-hand one with *R.* 'Sander's White Rambler'.

orange and red heleniums and 'Hidcote Pink' penstemons (a favourite of Barry's). *Macleaya cordata* 'Spetchley Ruby' gives height and softness.

At the end is a pebble mosaic and a plaque to Lavinia Cholmondeley in tribute to her horticultural dedication and creativity: 'Hortorum creatrix, 1921–2015'. Beyond a semi-circle of hornbeam lie the Rockery and the Temple Garden. Lady Lavinia made the rockery, cascade and the bridge over the lake, whose banks are covered with snowdrops, crocus and daffodils from January. Marginal planting includes *Darmera peltata*, a good-value plant with primula-like pink flowers on stalks in spring before its scalloped leaves emerge. *Darmera* gives excellent summer structure and autumn colour, as does the fern *Osmunda regalis*, along with *Acer rubrum* and the deciduous *Taxodium distichum* on the banks.

Beyond, the parkland's 250 acres include the arboretum, Tower Hill and woodlands walks. The Folly Garden was planted in 2006 with the help of accomplished designer Xa Tollemache. Here, Himalayan varieties of hydrangea, the rusty foxglove, *Digitalis ferruginea*, and the Tibetan cowslip, *Primula florindae*, thrive in the shady conditions. But as with all good gardens, developments continue; plants are often moved to find their right place, for, as Barry concludes: 'If they have to work too hard for their living, you shouldn't have them.' Further work in the Folly Garden in 2016 cleared laurel and scrubby overgrowth and allowed for further planting opportunities, while opening up new views of this constantly evolving garden.

Holker Hall, Cumbria

The entrance to Holker Hall and its gardens is through classic English parkland that rolls away towards the majestic Lake District mountains. You enter ornamental gardens near the house only to be enticed out again through hedged compartments of topiary. The 25 acres of gardens and grounds fit together like hand in glove, and even in the most enclosed of the formal areas you are aware of the wider parkland.

In spring, bulbs fill the beds, while magnolias, rhododendrons and azaleas bloom in the woodland's acidic soil. Arrive in June to be intoxicated by the scent of the Lime Walk beside the wildflower meadow. By the time the garden closes for the season at the end of October, woodland and parkland have turned golden and the topiary is white with the first frosts.

Holker has never been sold since George Preston built a house here in 1603 on land owned by Cartmel Priory before the Dissolution of the Monasteries. It passed by inheritance to the Lowther family and then to the Cavendishes in the 1740s, in whose hands it remains. The present house was rebuilt in Elizabethan style in the 1870s after fire destroyed most of Preston's original mansion. The remaining wing is echoed, but in red sandstone quarried locally and embellished by Victorian turrets, towers and Gothic gables.

Similarly, old and new are united in the gardens. The cascade, built by Lord and Lady Cavendish (Hugh and Grania) in 1991, runs down towards the fountain and pool that were features of the original 1700s garden. Box, yew and beech in the Elliptical and Summer Gardens, recall formal gardens laid out by Sir Thomas Lowther in the 1720s.

Lord and Lady Cavendish did much else to enhance the gardens. In the 1990s, according to Matthew Murgatroyd, head gardener from September 2022, 'they stole the wildflower meadow from the parkland'. It is now integral to the garden, managed with a cutting regime that encourages the increase of wildflower species. Paths cut through the meadow lead to a labyrinth of slate uprights inspired by Lake District stone circles. Another path goes to a slate sundial, designed by Sir Mark Lennox-

The effect of the Arts and Crafts movement can be seen in the Sunken Garden. It was designed in the early 1900s by Thomas Mawson, whose book *The Art and Craft of Garden Making* influenced Lawrence Johnston at Hidcote (see pp. 82–86). Other examples of the gardens' Arts and Crafts character are the use of local slate in the paths, with borders of pebbles hand-selected by Lord and Lady Cavendish themselves. Four benches in the Elliptical Garden are each made from slate mined from a different Cavendish quarry. Their varied textures are set against semi-circular beds of roses, perennials and annual *Lavandula pinnata*.

Clipped columns, domes, wedges and cubes abound: in the Summer Garden, yew spirals stand on box bases and square-topped hawthorns (with crowns of white in May) within yew plinths. Buttresses of yew with top-knots like iced gems divide up sections planted with dahlias, agapanthus, sedums, knautia, nepeta and black elder in the long bed of the Summer Garden. A weeping pear (*Pyrus salicifolia* 'Pendula') stands in each of four willow-edged beds connected by tunnels of Portuguese laurel.

Boyd, and looking as though it has erupted naturally from the stone beneath.

Another innovation is the Pagan Grove, a sunken ellipse designed by landscape architect Kim Wilkie as a contrast to the shadier woodland and the formal gardens. Around its rim are specimen trees: a mulberry, the August-flowering *Catalpa bignonioides*, a fastigiate beech, eucryphia and katsura tree *Cercidiphyllum japonicum*. Older trees nearby include a magnificent cut-leaf beech and the rugged, spreading, 400-year-old Great Lime. By the pool is the monkey puzzle tree (*Araucaria araucana*), grown from seed given in 1844 by plant collector William Lobb to Joseph Paxton, head gardener at Chatsworth and architect of Crystal Palace.

Buttresses of yew with top-knots like iced gems divide up sections planted with dahlias, agapanthus, sedums, knautia, nepeta and black elder in the long bed of the Summer Garden.

Opposite A black wrought-iron gate has recently been introduced by Holker's new chatelaine, Lady Lucy Cavendish, and opens from the Summer Garden onto a mown path through the wildflower meadow.

Above The towers of Holker Hall can be seen across the wildflower meadow in which stands the labyrinth. It is composed of slate uprights inspired by Lake District stone circles such as Castlerigg near Keswick.

Left Sculpted yews give year-round structure and a strong green background to planting in the Elliptical Garden. In spring, the yews are bordered by pure white daffodils, including *Narcissus* 'Thalia'.

Linking the Summer and Elliptical Gardens are pleached limes, a tunnel of 'Lord Lambourne' apples and yew arches; in between are compartments brimming with *Alchemilla mollis*. Matthew smilingly says the garden is 'almost overplanted in places', but he particularly likes repetition both in the bedding (for instance, of *Verbena bonariensis* and *V. rigida* 'Santos Purple' used as annuals) and in more structural planting. Whitebeams recur: in the Elliptical Garden, the parkland is seen between the trunks of two loosely clipped *Sorbus aria* 'Lutescens'. An avenue of ten *S. a.* 'Magnifica', planted in December 2022, give interest from spring flowers through silvery foliage in summer to berries and strong colour in autumn.

Since 2015, the Cavendishes' daughter, Lucy, has been in charge. An early move has been to erect a black wrought-iron gate in the hornbeam hedge of the Summer Garden to hint at what lies beyond. Encouraging visitors to explore every inch of garden and parkland is very much what Holker does.

Above Phlox, sedums, campanulas and other perennials swirl around a weeping pear in the beds of the Sunken Garden. Roses along the back wall hark back to the original planting by Arts and Crafts designer Thomas Mawson, who laid out this garden in the early 20th century.

Left Lord Cavendish is a patron of the European Boxwood and Topiary Society, so clipped box and yew play an important part in the garden immediately around the hall. Stepped box is flanked by banks of lavender with a lead trough filled with summer bedding behind.

Below *Teucrium fruticans* edges the paths through the Summer Garden. At the centre of the garden, four weeping pears (*Pyrus salicifolia* 'Pendula') stand in willow-framed beds, in which summer bedding replaces spring tulips.

Kiftsgate Court Gardens, Gloucestershire

From its hilltop, Kiftsgate Court in Gloucestershire looks outward between Scots and Monterey pines. The panorama over the Vale of Evesham towards Bredon Hill and the Malverns is the ever-present background to garden rooms hedged by yew, holly and beech and filled with colour and scent.

That view inspired the garden's creator, Heather Muir, and her husband, Jack, to buy Kiftsgate in 1919, possibly encouraged by Lawrence Johnston, their next door neighbour at Hidcote (see pp. 82–86). Heather had no knowledge of horticulture or design, yet, on a narrow plateau and on banks plummeting 100 foot, she laid out one of Britain's most bewitching gardens. Kiftsgate has been tended in turn by Heather's daughter, Diany Binny, and, since 1988, by Diany's daughter, Anne Chambers, and her husband, Johnny. Each generation has kept faith with Heather's creation.

Kiftsgate was a garden of its time with specimen trees, shrubs, perennials and roses, and a soft colour palette. When shrubs went out of fashion to be replaced by grasses, perennials and drought-tolerant groundcover, Anne continued to garden as her mother and grandmother had done. 'We still look back at plants that remind us of earlier generations,' says Anne, 'but we introduce new species and cultivars.' There have been some adaptations, such as the very sparing use of grasses: a rosy line of *Pennisetum thunbergii* 'Red Buttons' beside the entrance path picks up the colour of a berberis hedge. Anne's approach has given Kiftsgate a pleasing freshness and vitality.

Shrubs and trees work in step with flowery perennials in every bed. In the Wide Border, mounds of *Geranium* 'Brookside', *Nepeta* 'Blue Dragon', *Stachys byzantina* and *Dictamnus albus* var. *purpureus* are interspersed with *Gladiolus communis* subsp. *byzantinus*, roses 'Vanity' and 'Highdownensis' and sprays of white *Crambe cordifolia*. This 'ordered profusion', in Anne's words, is given definition by deutzias, hebes,

Shrubs and trees work in step with flowery perennials in every bed.

bay and domes of dwarf lilac, *Syringa meyeri* 'Palibin'. The same lilac reappears in the Four Squares folded into a corner of the house, and divided by stone paths along with bushy *Lonicera periclymenum* and wispy indigofera. These beds are planted with pale pink and lilac roses, peonies, salvias and geraniums.

Plants are used individually but frequently to create coherence between the various areas. Seeing the same plants in several contexts sets up different associations and highlights each one's qualities. The papery white flowers of summer-flowering, evergreen shrub *Carpenteria californica* are surrounded by colour in the Wide Border, but in the White Sunk Garden are complemented by scented white *Philadelphus microphyllus* and eucryphia. *Deutzia setchuenensis* var. *corymbiflora* appears here and in the Lower Garden where its foliage contrasts with Mediterranean planting.

The Lower Garden lies below the towering Banks, terraced by Italian gardeners in the 1930s. Shaded by those vast, view-defining

Monterey pines, ceanothus, senecio, cistus and viburnums benefit from dry soil and the south-west aspect. Frosts roll over the top, leaving unscathed the more tender, pale mauve *Abutilon vitifolium* and *Hebe hulkeana*, a New Zealand native. The look here is very different but is linked with the flowery beds on the plateau above by tree and lactiflora peonies, a China *Rosa × odorata* 'Bengal Crimson' and olearias.

Back on the plateau and running away from the house, the Rose Border is defined by knee-high hedges of *Rosa gallica* 'Versicolor' surrounded by old roses in pinks to deep reds. Their season is June and early July when the garden's eponymous monster *R. filipes* 'Kiftsgate' also reaches its peak – a mass of creamy, musk-scented blooms. Heather planted the rose in 1938 as a backdrop to the border, little expecting it to skyrocket above a nearby copper beech. It was identified in the 1950s by rosarian Graham Stuart Thomas as *R. filipes* and named for the garden.

Amid the pastels are stronger notes. Within the berberis hedge and *Cotinus coggygria* 'Royal

Above The White Sunk Garden predated Sissinghurst's more famous White Garden by 20 years. In early summer, it is encircled by flowering shrubs including *Staphylea colchica*, *Carpenteria californica*, deutzias and *Philadelphus microphyllus*.

Purple', the Red Border features *Penstemon* 'Chester Scarlet', *Heuchera* 'Palace Purple' and *Dahlia* 'Bishop of Llandaff'. The Yellow Border, glittering with bronze, blues, lime and egg-yolk yellows, displays the work of all three generations. Heather set the tone with the gold *Acer shirasawanum* 'Aureum' and the mahogany *A. palmatum* 'Dissectum Atropurpureum', beneath which Diany added a tier of colour-echoing shrubs including *Cotinus coggygria* 'Royal Purple' and *Berberis thunbergii* 'Aurea' along with yellow Molly-the-Witch peonies and delphiniums. Anne's contribution has been punchy orange 'Ballerina' tulips, which successfully repeat each year.

The Chambers created the Water Garden in 1999–2000 on a former tennis court: its fountain of gilded philodendron leaves gently swaying over a discreet, dark pool. It is now the garden's green lungs. The spoil was later used for the rugosa rose-covered mound outside the formal garden. Anne and Johnny have enjoyed building on her mother's and grandmother's achievements over 35 years. 'I have always known this garden,' Anne says, 'but I have never taken it for granted.'

Right The gilded bronze philodendron fountain of the Water Garden can be glimpsed from the Fern Border through a gap in the yew hedging. Created in 1990–2000, this green garden has become the still heart of Kiftsgate.

Below In the Four Squares, the rare pink and dazzling *Rosa* 'Rita' stands out among exuberant planting of long-flowering *Deutzia setchuenensis* var. *corymbiflora*, a bush honeysuckle, *Geranium robustum* and *Indigofera pendula*.

Newby Hall, North Yorkshire

In the late 17th century, Celia Fiennes travelled the country on horseback, recording her observations in diaries that were later published. In them, this remarkable woman described Newby Hall as the most beautiful house in Yorkshire. This Hampton Court Palace in miniature was designed in the 1680s by Sir Christopher Wren for Sir Edward Blackett, MP for Ripon. Were Celia Fiennes to return, she would certainly be impressed by how well house and garden now complement each other.

The garden was laid out by Major Edward Compton, a descendant of William Weddell whose family bought the estate in 1748. When Newby was left to Edward by his mother, Mary, in 1921, he wrote: 'I had inherited an exceptionally beautiful home but no garden to speak of – a lovely picture but no frame.' All that existed was William Burges's 1880 Statue Walk with yew drums and Venetian statues; Victorian parterres near the house; and the Rock Garden, completed in 1914 under the guidance of Ellen Willmott (the legendarily extravagant gardener who ordered an alpine garden for her 21st birthday).

Influenced by Lawrence Johnston's work at Hidcote in Gloucestershire (see pp. 82–86), Edward structured the garden, beginning by planting windbreak blocks of woodlands mainly to the west and south-west. Small pockets of Portuguese laurel, yew and holly were planted within the garden, some of which survive. Mature pines and deciduous trees now envelop the garden's fabulous display of over 50 magnolias, 40 flowering cherries, countless species of summer flowering shrubs (including a National Collection of Cornus) and herbaceous perennials.

Of the Victorian parterres, Edward retained only a stone balustrade by the Lily Pond to the south front of the house. Below, a green room of yew platforms and monumental stone urns opens on to 564-foot herbaceous borders that form a grand Italianate vista down to the River Ure. These borders, the longest in a private garden in Britain, were created in the 1930s and redesigned in 2013 after a three-year research project, led by Lucinda Compton, the garden's curator and wife of the current owner, Richard. 'Family involvement helps shape the

Above Newby Hall holds a National Collection of *Cornus*, including *Cornus kousa* 'Miss Satomi', *C. kousa* 'Milky Way' and *C. kousa* 'Greensleeves'. The Rose Garden fountain is visible beyond a pair of terracotta urns.

Left One of the Millennium Beacons, commissioned by councils across the UK, was given a home at Newby Hall, replacing a copper beech felled by honey fungus. It is surrounded by weeping pears (*Pyrus salicifolia* 'Pendula'), spring-flowering magnolias and a collection of peonies.

Opposite The 564-foot herbaceous borders, leading from the house to the River Ure, are the centrepiece of Newby Hall's garden. Backed by yew hedging and parkland trees, they are an undulating and ever-changing river of colour.

garden,' she says. 'It doesn't get set in stone, for each generation makes a contribution.' The planting in borders backed by yew is bright and contemporary, yet preserves the traditional country house look. The colour palette (blues, pinks, reds, silver and spikes of pale yellow and cream) is inspired by the tree-scape above the hedges. 'This links the border into the garden,' explains Lucinda, 'rather than it being stand-alone planting.' The planting is asymmetrical left to right and non-rhythmic in its repetition. Planting drifts and combinations are equally effective whether viewed along the border's length or diagonally. Looked at directly, the borders appear as a series of 'stills'. Key plants are euphorbia to inject acid green, feathery *Datisca cannabina*, *Onopordum acanthium*, *Ageratina altissima* 'Chocolate' and asters in all their guises.

Planted in five blocks each side and 13-foot deep, these borders are the garden's spine. There is some symmetry across them between the Rose Garden on one side and the Autumn

Old and modern shrub roses are underplanted with summer perennials, and other highlights include daphne, tree peonies and clematis.

Garden on the other, each with central fountain and pool. *Rosa* 'Felicia' and 'Buff Beauty' line the path to the sunken pink and silver Rose Garden, designed within copper beech hedging by Edward in the 1930s. Old and modern shrub roses are underplanted with summer perennials, and other highlights include daphne, tree peonies and clematis. In the Autumn Garden, hibiscus stand in beds with over 50 species and cultivars of salvias (lifted and replanted each year), 12 dahlia cultivars and late summer crocosmia, hydrangeas and red monardas.

Gardens, such as Robin's Walk, are named for family members. This short, double herbaceous border of blues and yellows was made in 2008 by Robin Compton, Edward's son and Lucinda's father-in-law. 'A passion for horticulture has been handed down,' says Lucinda. 'I have lived in the house for 23 years and was taught by Robin, who adored the garden.'

Robin's Walk leads into Sylvia's Garden, a memorial to Edward's wife, who died in 1950. Stone and brick paths meet at a Byzantine corn grinder encircled by four standard *Rosa* 'Ballerina'. Four coralberries (*Symphoricarpos orbiculatus* 'Variegatus') and clipped box give structure to looser pastel planting of annuals and perennials.

There are wooded areas, wildflower banks, a grove of cornus and a water garden with primulas, hostas, gunnera, astilbe, ligularia and bamboo. After a century of neglect, a £100,000 redevelopment programme began in 2019 on the Rock Garden, which covers over 5,250 square feet. Here, a metasequoia and swamp cypress (*Taxodium distichum*) tower over bridges and stepping stones, arches, pools, rills and craggy rocks pocketed by alpines.

In the ebb and flow between the open and the enclosed, you sense the family at work. Lucinda and Lawrence Wright, head gardener since October 2021, walk round the garden together every week. 'Furloughing the gardeners during Covid made me more hands on and increased my knowledge of the garden,' says Lucinda. She pays tribute to Lawrence, who 'has completely changed the underplanting in the Rose Garden, introduced new plants to the Autumn Garden, and used *Lilium* 'Sweet Surrender' to great effect between Sylvia's Garden and Robin's Walk.' 'This is an amazing garden,' says Lawrence, 'but there is always room for change.' He is currently working on a further redesign of planting in the Rock Garden, before starting on the Tropical Garden. It is clear that Newby will continue to honour its past while maintaining unstoppable momentum.

Gardens to visit

Bodnant, Tal-y-Cafn, Conwy LL28 5RE (nationaltrust.org.uk/bodnant-garden)

Borde Hill, Borde Hill Lane, Haywards Heath, West Sussex RH16 1XP (bordehill.co.uk)

Bourton House Garden, Bourton-on-the-Hill, Glos GL56 9AE (bourtonhouse.com)

Branklyn Garden, 116 Dundee Road, Perth PH2 7BB (nts.org.uk/visit/places/branklyn-garden)

Brantwood, East of Lake, Coniston, Cumbria LA21 8AD (brantwood.org.uk)

Caerhays Castle, Gorran, St Austell, Cornwall PL26 6LY (visit.caerhays.co.uk)

Cholmondeley Castle Gardens, Malpas, Cheshire SY14 8ET (cholmondeleycastle.com)

East Ruston Old Vicarage, East Ruston, Norwich, Norfolk NR12 9HN (eastrustonoldvicarage.co.uk)

Felbrigg Hall, near Cromer, Norfolk NR11 8PP (nationaltrust.org.uk/felbrigg)

Glendurgan Garden, Mawnan Smith, near Falmouth, Cornwall TR11 5JZ (nationaltrust.org.uk/glendurgan)

Great Dixter House & Gardens, Northiam, Rye, East Sussex TN31 6PH (greatdixter.co.uk)

Hidcote, near Chipping Campden, Glos GL55 6LR (nationaltrust.org.uk/hidcote)

Holehird Gardens, Patterdale Road, Windermere, Cumbria LA23 1NP (holehirdgardens.org.uk)

Holker Hall, Cark-in-Cartmel, Grange-over-Sands, Cumbria LA11 7PL (holker.co.uk)

Kiftsgate Court Gardens, near Chipping Campden, Glos GL55 6LN (kiftsgate.co.uk)

Lamorran House Gardens, Upper Castle Road, St Mawes, Cornwall TR2 5BZ (lamorrangardens.co.uk)

Levens Hall, Kendal, Cumbria LA8 0PD (levenshall.co.uk)

Llanerchaeron, Ciliau Aeron, near Aberaeron, Ceredigion SA48 8DG (nationaltrust.org.uk/llanerchaeron)

Mottisfont, near Romsey, Hampshire SO51 0LP (nationaltrust.org.uk/mottisfont)

Mount Stewart, Portaferry Road, Newtownards, Co. Down BT22 2AD (nationaltrust.org.uk/mount-stewart)

Newby Hall & Gardens, Ripon, North Yorkshire HG4 5AE (newbyhall.com)

Nymans, Handcross, near Haywards Heath, West Sussex RH17 6EB (nationaltrust.org.uk/nymans)

Overbeck's Garden, Sharpitor, Salcombe, Devon TQ8 8LW (nationaltrust.org.uk/overbecks)

Packwood House, Packwood Lane, Lapworth, Warwicks B94 6AT (nationaltrust.org.uk/packwood)

Polesden Lacey, Great Bookham, Surrey RH5 6BD (nationaltrust.org.uk/polesden-lacey)

Powis Castle, Welshpool, Powys SY21 8RF (nationaltrust.org.uk/powis)

Scampston, Malton, North Yorkshire YO17 8NG (scampston.co.uk)

Sissinghurst Castle Garden, Biddenden Road, near Cranbrook, Kent N17 2AB (nationaltrust.org.uk/sissinghurst)

The Trentham Estate, Stone Road, Trentham, Stoke-on-Trent, Staffs ST4 8JG (threntham.co.uk)

Wallington, Cambo, near Morpeth, Northumberland NE61 4AR (nationaltrust.org.uk/wallington)

Wildside, Green Lane, Buckland Monachorum, Devon PL20 7NP (wileyatwildside.com)

Wollerton Old Hall Garden, Wollerton, Market Drayton, Shropshire TF9 3NA (wollertonoldhallgarden.com)

Index

Picture credits

Front cover: Mount Stewart, County Down (©National Trust Images/James Dobson). Back cover, top left: Sissinghurst Castle Garden, Kent (©National Trust Images/Annaick Guitteny). Back cover, top right: Wollerton Old Hall, Shropshire (©Joe Wainwright). Back cover, bottom: Holker Hall, Cumbria (©Joe Wainwright).

2: ©National Trust Images/James Dobson. 4, 7, 8: ©Joe Wainwright. 9 top: ©National Trust Images/James Dobson. 9 bottom: ©Joe Wainwright. 10: ©Jason Ingram. 11: ©National Trust Images/James Dobson. 12–13: ©Joe Wainwright. 14, 16, 17, 18, 19: ©GAP Photos/John Glover. 21, 22, 23, 24, 26, 27, 28, 29, 30, 31, 32, 33: ©National Trust Images/James Dobson. 35, 36, 37, 38, 39: ©National Trust Images/Annaick Guitteny. 40, 41, 42, 43: ©Joe Wainwright. 44–45, 47, 48, 49, 50, 51: ©National Trust Images/Joe Wainwright. 52, 54, 55, 56: ©Ray Cox Photography. 57, 58, 59, 60, 61: ©National Trust Images/Jason Ingram. 63, 64, 65, 66: ©Joe Wainwright. 67, 68, 69, 70: ©Mark Bolton Photography. 71, 72, 73, 74, 75: ©National Trust Images/Jason Ingram. 76–77, 79, 80, 81, 82, 84, 85, 86, 87, 88, 89, 90: ©National Trust Images/James Dobson. 91, 92, 93, 94: ©GAP Photos/Rob and Jo Whitworth. 95, 96, 97, 98, 99: ©National Trust Images/James Dobson. 100–101, 103, 104, 105, 106, 107, 108, 109, 110: ©Joe Wainwright. 111, 112, 113, 114, 115, 117, 118, 119, 120: ©National Trust Images/James Dobson. 121, 122, 123, 124, 125: ©National Trust Images/Joe Wainwright. 126–127: ©Joe Wainwright. 128, 130, 131, 132: ©Mandy Bradshaw. 133, 134, 135, 136, 137: ©Richard Bloom. 139, 140, 141, 142: ©Joe Wainwright. 143, 144, 145, 146, 147: ©Jason Ingram. 148–149: ©Julie Skelton. 150: ©Nicky Flint. 152: ©Clive Nichols. 153 top: ©GAP Photos/John Glover. 153 bottom: ©Molly Hollman. 154: ©GAP Photos/John Glover. 155, 156, 157, 158, 159: ©Mark Bolton Photography. 160, 162, 163, 164, 165, 166, 168, 169, 170, 171: ©Joe Wainwright. 173, 174, 175, 176, 177: ©Sabina Rüber. 179, 180 bottom: ©Tom Marshall. 180 top, 181, 182: ©GAP Photos/Ellen Rooney.

For my sons, Nicholas and Matthew Evans,
who spent their childhood visiting gardens

Acknowledgements

First and foremost, I owe an enormous debt to the owners, head gardeners and gardeners of the 32 gardens all of whom feature in this book. They gave unstintingly of their time both when I visited and subsequently in reading my accounts and checking the captions. Without their help, this book would not have been possible. I am grateful, too, to the people behind the scenes who helped to fix up my interviews and to track down the gardeners (often elusive, by the very nature of their occupation). They include Lucinda Rimmington at Caerhays, Kathryn Skerratt at Cholmondeley Castle, Julie Rose at Bourton House, Mary-Anne Brightwell at Great Dixter, Olivia Jones and Clarissa Price for the National Trust in Wales, and Katie Spaven at Scampston.

I am equally grateful to Claire Masset at the National Trust and Peter Taylor at HarperCollins, who, by commissioning me to write this book, sent me on a year-long journey of discovery and initiated all the wonderful and instructive conversations I enjoyed in the process.

At HarperCollins, managing editor David Salmo has been a joy to work with throughout the editing process. My thanks also go to Lisa Footitt for her work on the index and to proof-reader, Katie Hewett, for her eagle eye. Ruby Tyler at the National Trust did an outstanding job on the picture research and on liaising with the photographers (unfortunately, too numerous to thank individually by name here) whose pictures have made the book look so lovely.

And thanks, too, to friends and family who hosted me as I travelled round the UK: Nicholas and Billy Evans and Sophie Williams, Matthew and Dougie Evans and Helena Moore, Kate Gibson, Linda Nicholson and Patrick Williams, Susan and Bob Tyson and Julia Watson.

Finally, and as ever, I want to pay tribute to the constant support of my husband, Chris Evans, my companion on many of the visits and my first and best reader.

Vanessa Berridge launched *The English Garden* magazine and is now an internationally published freelance writer on gardening and garden history. Her books have included *Great British Gardeners: From Early Plantsmen to Chelsea Medal Winners* (2018) and *Borde Hill Garden: A Plant Hunter's Paradise* (2022). *Kiftsgate Court Gardens: Three Generations of Women Gardeners* was the 2019 Garden Media Guild Book of the Year. Vanessa is the county organiser for the National Garden Scheme in Gloucestershire, where she lives and opens her garden for the charity.